Team Academy in Practice

Within entrepreneurship education, Team Academy is seen by some as an innovative pedagogical model that enhances social connectivity, as well as experiential, student-centred, and team-based learning. It also creates spaces for transformative learning to occur.

This second book of the Routledge Focus on Team Academy book series includes chapters from contributors working with the TA methodology in academic institutions around the world that discuss the challenges, benefits, and approaches to embedding the TA methodology in practice (around coaching, assessment, transformative learning, partnerships, programme evolution, etc.).

This book is aimed at academics, practitioners, and learners engaged in the Team Academy methodology, pedagogy, and model, as well as those interested in the area of entrepreneurial team learning. Readers will be inspired to innovate in their delivery methodologies and to explore learning-by-doing approaches to creating value. The book also aims to challenge the discourse around entrepreneurship and entrepreneurial activities, offering insights, research, stories, and experiences from those learning and working in the Team Academy approach.

Dr Berrbizne Urzelai is Team Coach and Senior Lecturer in areas of International Management and Entrepreneurship at the University of the West of England, UK.

Dr Elinor Vettraino is Head Coach and Programme Director of the Business Enterprise Development portfolio at Aston University, UK.

Routledge Focus on Team Academy
Series Editors – Berrbizne Urzelai and Elinor Vettraino

Higher Education organizations (HE) operate in an environment that continuously pushes towards innovation by educators. From this perspective, Team Academy is seen as an innovative pedagogical model that enhances social connectivity, as well as experiential, student-centred, and team-based learning. It also creates spaces for transformative learning to occur. Since its creation in Finland in 1993, the number of institutions adopting this approach has been expanding in many parts of Europe and beyond, and it is increasingly attracting the interest of organizations that want to adopt a model that emphasizes the transversal competences and skills acquired by its entrepreneurial learners. The aim of this series is to compile the different research, experiences, and stories about the Team Academy phenomenon throughout its worldwide network.

The audience of the books is multidisciplinary, directed to academics and practitioners. Entrepreneurial education and research has traditionally been focused on the individual entrepreneur. However, in the current business scenario, entrepreneurs' teamwork efforts, social capital, and networking skills are essential to face the entrepreneurial issues and challenges that they currently face. The books adopt a Team Academy pedagogical approach that focuses on critical factors such as team and experiential learning, leadership, or entrepreneurial mindset, which makes this collection a key information source for those looking at new directions of entrepreneurship education and practice.

Team Academy and Entrepreneurship Education
Edited by Elinor Vettraino and Berrbizne Urzelai

Team Academy in Practice
Edited by Berrbizne Urzelai and Elinor Vettraino

Team Academy: Leadership and Teams
Edited by Elinor Vettraino and Berrbizne Urzelai

Team Academy in Diverse Settings
Edited by Berrbizne Urzelai and Elinor Vettraino

Team Academy in Practice

Edited by Berrbizne Urzelai and Elinor Vettraino

Routledge
Taylor & Francis Group

NEW YORK AND LONDON

First published 2022
by Routledge
605 Third Avenue, New York, NY 10158

and by Routledge
4 Park Square, Milton Park, Abingdon, Oxon, OX14 4RN

*Routledge is an imprint of the Taylor & Francis Group, an
informa business*

Library of Congress Cataloguing-in-Publication Data
A catalogue record for this title has been requested

ISBN: 978-0-367-75595-9 (hbk)
ISBN: 978-0-367-75596-6 (pbk)
ISBN: 978-1-003-16311-4 (ebk)

DOI: 10.4324/9781003163114

Typeset in Times New Roman
by MPS Limited, Dehradun

To my colleagues from Mondragon, Valencia, and UWE.
Thank you for stimulating my hunger for learning.

- Dr Berrbizne Urzelai

For the first pancake, I helped to cook - Dominique, Faye,
Sophie, Matthew, Jordan, and Raif. Thank you for the learning.

- Dr Elinor Vettraino

Contents

Figures

Tables

Acknowledgements

We would like to thank all of the contributors for their stories, and the learners, researchers, and practitioners for their commitment to exploration and learning-by-doing. Without them, this book wouldn't have been possible.

Dr Berrbizne Urzelai and Dr Elinor Vettraino

Contributors

Berrbizne Urzelai, Team Coach, and Senior Lecturer, University of West of England, UK: Dr. Berrbizne Urzelai is Team Coach and Senior Lecturer at the University of the West of England (UWE), Bristol (UK). Her teaching and research work is on Strategic Management, International Business, and Entrepreneurship. She holds an international PhD (Hons) in Economics and Business Management (University of Valencia), an MSc in East Asian Studies (University of Bristol), and an MBA (Mondragon University). She is also a Fellow of HEA. She has experience in working at different institutions applying for Team Academy programmes in different countries. Her research is related to international business, agglomeration economies, social capital, and knowledge management as well as TA-related country and model comparisons. Her research has received several awards (best paper 2017 XXVII ACEDE, best doctoral communication 2015 Torrecid, PhD. Scholarship, etc.). She is a member of different research groups, GESTOR (Organizational Geostrategy: Clusters and Competitiveness) at the University of Valencia and BLCC (Bristol Leadership and Change Centre) at UWE. Publications available here: https://people.uwe.ac.uk/Person/Berrbizne2Urzelai.

Elinor Vettraino, Programme Director and Head Coach, Aston University, UK: Dr. Elinor Vettraino is Head Coach and Programme Director of the Business Enterprise Development portfolio at Aston University, Birmingham, (UK). She also leads the Aston Business Clinic. She is the Founder and Director of Active Imagining, an organizational development, and leadership consultancy. She is also a Director of Akatemia UK through which she runs training for academics, consultants, and practitioners who are developing a programme of learning based on the principles of the Team Academy model. Elinor has a DEd Psychology (University of Dundee) and is a Senior Fellow of HEA, and a Chartered Fellow/Chartered Manager of CMI. Her research is currently based on understanding how the Team Academy model supports transformational learning for participants, and how the application of arts-based pedagogies might support the development of negative capability in team coaches and team entrepreneurs.

Colin Jones, Associate Professor, and Senior Academic Developer, University of Southern Queensland: Associate Professor Colin Jones is a Senior Academic Developer at the University of Southern Queensland (USQ). During the last 20 years, Colin has been a strong advocate for innovative approaches to enterprise and entrepreneurship education, and education more generally. The focus of Colin's research is on the development of student agency, transformative learning, signature pedagogies, the scholarship of teaching and learning (SoTL), firm survival, and ecological approaches to social phenomena. Colin currently is interested in exploring the limitations placed on learning by the actions of educators.

Lauren Davies, Lecturer, University of West of England, UK: Lauren (MSc, BA (Hons), FHEA, FIEEP) is a Director of Enterprise Educators UK and a Lecturer in Enterprise and Entrepreneurship/ Team Coach at the University of the West of England. Lauren's role involves coaching a team of undergraduate students on the Team Entrepreneurship programme, adopting the innovative Team Academy model of team-based, experiential, self-managed entrepreneurial learning. Lauren worked alongside the Programme Lead on the revalidation of the programme in 2019–20, launching a new programme design in 2020. Lauren also teaches on Enterprise and Entrepreneurship, a first-year undergraduate module within the Business Management pathways with circa 1000 students enroled. Her experience thus ranges from delivering a specialist entrepreneurship education programme to large-scale entrepreneurship education delivery.

Antoine Perruchoud, Professor HES, Head of Team Academy HES-SO, HES-SO Valais-Wallis, Switzerland: Professor HES, Head of HES-SO Team Academy and Delegate professor of the faculty economy and services for the Master Innokick at HES-SO. Antoine Perruchoud is an academic and practitioner with years of interest and experience in developing and teaching innovation, business models and entrepreneurship. He initially studied at the Swiss University of Fribourg (BA in Business Administration) and afterwards at the US Western Washington University (MSc in sustainable development). He moved on to become a scientific collaborator at the Swiss Federal Agency for the Environment. Following this Antoine started as a professor at the HES-SO Valais. Here he initiated a new entrepreneurship programme: Business Experience. In the Master of Advanced Studies "Quality & Strategy Management", he has been responsible for the course in Innovation Management since 2008. Lastly, Antoine launched in 2017 the first Team Academy bachelor in Switzerland: a disruptive pedagogical model based on "learning by doing" and "team learning". As co-founder of Keylemon.com and as a passionate snow sports instructor he always explores new business and "freeriding" opportunities.

Lionel Emery, Team Coach, and Academic collaborator: Lionel Emery obtained a Master in Business Administration (MSc, BA). In his master's work, he was interested in management practices and project management methods in startups and thus developed an expertise in these fields. He completed his training with a diploma in team coaching (Team Mastery, UK) performed in an international context (England and Finland). In 2017, he actively participated in the launch of the first Team Academy in Switzerland and is currently a team coach and academic collaborator within this programme. Lionel is also involved as a team coach with the students of the "Business eXperience" entrepreneurship training programme.

Olga Bourachnikova, Associate professor, Strasbourg Business School, University of Strasbourg, France: Olga Bourachnikova joined the Strasbourg Business School as an associate professor in Finance. The discovery of Team Academy in Finland led her to transform her professional career. In 2011, she co-created the Team Entrepreneur Bachelor programme she coordinates and team-coaches ever since. Her research subjects are related to the learning by doing and the teftanam learning pedagogical issues. Focused on the individual, she questions to what extent the Team Academy approach helps the student to become more autonomous and competent.

Caroline Merdinger-Rumpler, Associate professor, Strasbourg Business School, University of Strasbourg, France: Caroline Merdinger-Rumpler is an associate professor in Management Science at the

Business School of the University of Strasbourg. She is the coordinator of the post-professional "Management of Health and Medico-Social Organizations" Master's Degree. Her research interests mainly deal with strategic and organizational issues faced by Health Organizations (change management, marketing), with an extra focus on organizational human behaviours and patient/ employee empowerment. Her recent involvement in the Team Entrepreneur Bachelor programme as a team coach has led her to investigate more deeply learning and pedagogical research questions.

Polly Wardle, Head of Education, Bristol City Robins Foundation, UK: Polly Wardle is Head of Education at Bristol City Robins Foundation. In this role, Polly manages a department of 20 staff, accountable for over 200 students ranging from level 2 to degree programmes. Using the power of sport, particularly football, these programmes inspire learners who might not have flourished in traditional educational settings. Polly programme leads the BA (Hons) Sports Business and Entrepreneurship degree based at Ashton Gate stadium and has been a team coach on the programme for 4 years using the Team Academy methodology.

Nan Jiang, Senior Lecturer in Entrepreneurship, Coventry University London Campus, UK: Dr Nan Jiang is an award-winning entrepreneurship educator supporting students in experiential learning. As a team entrepreneurship coach, she supports young aspiring entrepreneurs in their venture creation process. She researches entrepreneurship education, enterprise practice, entrepreneurial identity construction strategy and family business succession. She works closely with accelerators, entrepreneurs, and industry partners to deliver the best learning experience to students that also add value to her research. She has presented research in academic conferences worldwide, such as Babson College Conference, British Academy of Management, and Institute for Small Business and Entrepreneurship. Her recent publications include an article in the International Journal of Small Business and a book chapter on Women's Involvement in Chinese family businesses.

Gabriel Faerstein, Team Coach, & Programme Manager, Team Academy Amsterdam, The Netherlands: Gabriel is passionate about Entrepreneurship, Education & Innovation. Since the beginning of his professional career, he has combined the three fields to contribute to a sustainable future. He has led my own ventures, consulted for corporates, scale-ups & governmental institutions, and finally team coaching and education management. In 2014, Gabriel moved from Brazil to The Netherlands, to follow the Team Academy Amsterdam programme. After graduating, he was invited to continue on as a Team Coach and a Programme Manager – further contributing to the impact of this innovative educational model.

Jose Maria Luzarraga Monasterio, Co-founder and team coach, MTA-Mondragon Unibertsitatea, Basque Country (Spain): Dr. Jose Mari Luzarraga is the Co-founder & alma mater of Mondragon Team Academy (MTA World www.MTAworld.com) & LEINN degree. He is an ASHOKA Fellow since December 2015. Senior lecturer at Mondragon University since 2004 lecturing in MBA and masters specialized in Global Business, co-operatives, social entrepreneurship & CSR strategies. International researcher of MIK (Mondragon Innovation Knowledge) research centre. Visiting professor at NEWSCHOOL from New York. Speaker at several international conferences in India, Norway, Chile, Mexico, Colombia, USA (World Bank Youth Summit), Saudi Arabia, China & Brazil, he has collaborated in research projects with different universities as CEIBS (Shanghai), Tecnologico de Monterrey (Mexico) or Harvard Business School (Boston). Serial social entrepreneur having co-founded several social business startups such as "Viaje Solidario" a responsible tourism platform (2004), Empathya Consulting: CSR & leadership consulting (2005), "EusKalAsia" Basque Country & Asia platform (2006), Mondragon Team Academy – MTA (2008), TZBZ innovation consultancy (2012), MTA China (2014), Impact HUB Shanghai (2016), INNKUBO BlockChain Technologies (2018), ABORA Ltd (2018), MTA Afrika S.Coop (2019), OX Riders Ltd electric motorbikes (2019). Advisory Board member of TZBZ S.Coop, DOT S.Coop, OX Riders Ltd.

Markel Gibert, CEO, Travelling U- Tazebaez, Basque Country (Spain): Team entrepreneur in Mondragon Team Academy and the first generation of LEINN degree. He co-founded Tazebaez S.coop. a Social Innovation Consultancy in 2012, where nowadays employ more than 40 people in a cooperative manner. Within this consultancy, he founded Travelling U in 2016, a disrupting learning platform, that creates a world campus for human potential. They run social innovation and entrepreneurship programmes in more than 5 countries, with open innovation laboratories in Shanghai, Seoul, Berlin, and Bilbao. Collaborative and cooperative human beings focused on launching different projects and businesses to create positive impact.

Berta Lazaro, Co-founder of Teamlabs, Team Labs, Spain: Co-founder of Teamlabs, education company since 2010. Learning and Innovation Facilitation Master LIT 2021, Humanity and Education Faculty University of Mondragon. 2021. Team Mastery Jyvaskyla University Finland, 2012. Urban Design Master University of Berkeley 2008. Architect from Navarra University 2002. Designer of team learning laboratories, freedom contexts to learn in teams through social impact projects that will generate great value for society. Working on the perimeters of different disciplines to diversify learning processes for institutions, organizations, companies, and people. Researching about real-life learning experiences, creating the "Learning by billing" methodology.

Aitor Lizartza, Academic Coordinator in Entrepreneurship, Mondragon Unibertsitatea, Basque Country (Spain): Aitor Lizartza is Doctor by Mondragon Unibertsitatea in business management with the thesis of "Key factors for the creation of biotech companies in the Basque country" since February 2009. He has participated in several research projects in entrepreneurship and innovation. International Master in Jyväskylä Applied Sciences University (Tiimiakatemia Finland). Co-founder of Mondragon Team Academy entrepreneurship unit in Mondragon University and design of the degree in entrepreneurial leadership and innovation (LEINN), verified by ANECA (Spanish accreditation entity) in 2009 and first official title on entrepreneurship (accredited in March 2017). From 2016 Mondragon Team Academy-Entrepreneurship Coordinator in Mondragon University (Faculty of Business).

Introduction
Team Academy in Practice

Berrbizne Urzelai and Elinor Vettraino

Team Academy: Philosophy, Pedagogy, and Process

Within Entrepreneurship Education, Team Academy (TA) is seen by some as an innovative pedagogical model that enhances social connectivity, as well as experiential (Kolb, 1984; Kayes, 2002), student-centred (Brandes & Ginnis, 1986), and team-based learning (Senge 1990). It also creates spaces for transformative learning to occur (Mezirow, 2008, 1991, 1998).

"If you really want to see the future of management education, you should see Team Academy," commented Peter Senge (2008) over a decade ago about TA and since its inception in JAMK - the university of applied sciences, Jyväskylä, Finland in the early 1990s, educators and practitioners engaging in TA based programmes have continuously pushed at the innovation boundaries of more traditional teaching approaches to education.

TA is often referred to as a model of entrepreneurship education. There are certain tools, techniques, and approaches that are used within the delivery of a TA-based programme that would support the idea of this being a framework or model that can be applied in different contexts. However, TA is a complex concept appearing not just as a model of activity, but as a pedagogical approach to learning and as a process of self (personal and professional) development. As a pedagogical approach, TA draws on the concept of heutagogical learning (Hase & Kenyon, 2001; Blaschke & Hase, 2016) to develop learners' capacity for self-determination in relation, not just to their academic work, but to their entrepreneurial ventures and their personal and professional development.

Since its creation, the number of institutions adopting this approach has been expanding in many parts of Europe and beyond, and it is increasingly attracting the interest of organizations that want to adopt

DOI: 10.4324/9781003163114-1

a model that emphasizes the transversal competences and skills acquired by its entrepreneurial learners.

Why This Book Series, and Why Now?

Berrbizne: The idea of publishing a Team Academy (TA) book for me started back in 2017 when I began working in the UK, because I could see that there were many differences between how TA was run in Mondragon (Basque Country) and at UWE (UK). In November that year, I met with an editor from Routledge and shared some of my ideas which he became excited about. However, it was not until March 2018 that I really started to put some ideas together for the project. I was already in touch with Elinor Vettraino, co-editor of this series, at that time as we were working on several cross-university projects and I remember a conversation I had with her over dinner in Finland in January 2018 (*Timmiakatemia*'s 25th Anniversary). Essentially, we were discussing why it was that not many people knew about TA even within our institutions. How could it be possible that we were not using the amazing global network more effectively?

Elinor: In June 2018, the Team Academy UK community had their annual meeting event – the TAUK Gathering. During this connection, a number of team coaches met and reflected together about how research could actually inform our team coaching practice, programme design, pedagogical thinking, etc. I was keen to organise a Team Learning Conference where we could invite people from TA but also other EE practitioners and academics to present their work and share their knowledge. At this point, Berrbizne and I realised that we had an opportunity to pool our interests together and publish a book for dissemination as well as organise a conference to share knowledge and practice.

Berrbizne: I was about to go on maternity leave so I thought … this is the moment! I need to do something during this time, so let's work on the book proposal. We created a call for chapters and started reaching out to people from our network to invite them to send us an abstract. The response was great and we ended up working on a proposal that had too many chapters so Routledge suggested a book series instead. We didn't want to leave people out of this so we thought *let's do it!*
    The rest, as they say, is history!

The Aim of the Series

Surprisingly there is very little published research about the theory and practice behind the Team Academy model so this book series aims to change that position. We have 4 main objectives through this project:

- Challenge the existing discourse around entrepreneurship, entre-preneurial activities, and enterprise education, and act as a provocation to generate new knowledge based on team learning and generating networks of teams.
- Collate research, narratives about practice, and the experiences of academics, team coaches, and team entrepreneurs who have worked with and through the Team Academy model of learning, and offer new insights to those engaged in developing entrepre-neurial education.
- Inspire academics and practitioners to innovate in their delivery methodologies and to explore learning-by-doing approaches to creating value.
- Show the diversity of approaches that exist within the TA network (different institutions, countries, designs, etc.).

We wanted to compile the different research, experiences, and stories about the Team Academy phenomenon throughout its worldwide network. This included research but also narrative journeys, reflec-tions, and student voices. This will allow us to get TA on the map when it comes to research as we wanted to show that because you work in TA doesn't mean you can't be a researcher.

There is not a single TA model as different institutions have applied this approach in different ways, so we wanted to celebrate the diversity within the model, and create an international network of practitioners and researchers that work around it. This will not only inform our practice but also offer it externally as something to be explored by other educators that is different from traditional learning and teaching models.

The Story of *Team Academy in Practice*

This second book of the *Routledge Focus on Team Academy* series collates research and stories about the experiences of academics and team coaches who have been driven by or worked with and through the Team Academy model of learning.

Programmes around the world implementing TA methods will explore how for instance, experiential learning, transformative learning, or competence-based learning is applied in their local contexts. Authors will discuss pedagogical designs in different settings, propose innovative assessment strategies, and reflect on how pedagogical factors influence, for instance, student motivation and engagement. The fact is that cooperative partnerships have made TA programmes grow and expand to different countries (i.e. China, India, Africa), disciplines (i.e. sport entrepreneurship), and levels (i.e. postgraduate degrees) but that expansion is not easy and often faces institutional barriers.

Throughout these war stories in this book, the readers will understand how that expansion was made possible, and which impact that had. The learnings from this book will also help the reader reflect on how the different TA programmes need to adapt to serve young team entrepreneurs that work in a *globally* interconnected world. This all will not be possible without the team coaches that support these learners throughout their journey of self-learning, real projects, and business. Thus, the book also includes a chapter around the training and development framework of team coaches that help comprehend the activity undertaken within this global TA system and leaves the opportunity for organizations to further build it based on their specific contexts.

References

Blaschke, L. M. & Hase, S. (2016). Heutagogy: A holistic framework for creating 21st century self-determined learners. In B. Gros and M. Maina Kinshuk (eds). *The future of ubiquitous learning: Learning designs for emerging pedagogies*, NYC: Springer, pp. 25–40.

Brandes, D. & Ginnis, P. (1986). *A guide to student centred learning*. Oxford: Blackwell.

Hase, S. & Kenyon, C. (2001). Moving from andragogy to heutagogy: Implications for VET. Proceedings of Research to Reality: Putting VET Research to Work: Australian Vocational Education and Training Research Association (AVETRA), Adelaide, SA, 28-30 March, AVETRA, Crows Nest, NSW.

Kayes, D. C. (2002). Experiential learning and its critics: Preserving the role of experience in management learning and education. *Academy of Management Learning & Education*, *1*(2), pp. 137–149. 10.5465/amle.2002.8509336

Kolb, D.A. (1984) *Experiential learning: Experience as the source of learning and development*. Englewood Cliffs, NJ: Prentice-Hall, Inc.

Mezirow, J. (1991). *Transformative dimensions of adult learning*. San Francisco: Jossey-Bass.

Mezirow, J. (1997). Transformative learning: Theory to practice. In P. Cranton (Ed.), Transformative learning in action. Vol. 74: *New directions for adult and continuing education* (pp. 5–12). San Francisco: Jossey-Bass.

Mezirow, J. (2008). An overview on transformative learning. *Lifelong learning*, 40–54.

Neck, H.M., Greene, P.G. & Brush, C.G. (2014). *Teaching entrepreneurship: A practice-based approach.* Edward Elgar, Cheltenham, UK.

Senge, P. (2008). Peter Senge - Team Academy. Tiimiakatemia Global Ltd, YouTube channel.

Senge, P. (1990). *Fifth discipline: The art and practice of the learning organisation.* London: Century.

1 On the Matter of Evidencing Transformative Learning in Enterprise/Entrepreneurship Education

Elinor Vettraino and Colin Jones

Introduction

It would seem to be widely believed that in the Higher Education context, enterprise/entrepreneurship education (hereinafter EE) can and should produce transformative learning outcomes (see Gibb, 1993; Hannon, 2005; Lourenco & Jones, 2006; Jones, 2019). Such views typically relate to the focus EE has on developing personal attributes, competencies, and deep changes in one's perspective of self and society. Disappointingly, there is very little empirical evidence confirming that transformative learning outcomes are common outcomes for students of EE. This dilemma is not entirely unique to EE, with the broader education literature also challenged around this issue. Indeed, it would seem easier to explain how transformative learning might occur than to evidence that it actually did occur (Taylor, 2007).

At the centre of this issue is the complex nature of transformational learning (hereinafter TL). *"Transformations may be epochal – sudden major reorientations in habit of mind, often associated with significant life crises or cumulative, a progressive sequence of insights resulting in changes in point of view and leading to a transformation in habit of mind"* (Mezirow, 2008, p. 28). The Mezirowian process of transformation is aligned to ten distinct stages, beginning with a disorienting dilemma, stages of critical self-examination, exploring and trying new roles, and developing self-confidence to facilitate the reintegration into one's life using newly gained perspectives.

However, a clear challenge in evidencing TL is recognizing that such learning outcomes are likely to occur via different experiences and learning processes, from one individual to the next. It is difficult to measure learning outcomes when the *"learner may skip one or more phases, return to a phase, or experience one phase in a more pronounced manner than another"* (Cox, 2017, p. 12). This article, set in the context

DOI: 10.4324/9781003163114-2

of EE, seeks to (1) explore the nature of TL, (2) consider the evidence that TL is widely occurring in EE before (3) providing empirical evidence of TL in an authentically unique EE context. The remainder of the paper is organized as follows. First, the literature on TL is considered, and the minimal requirements to support transformative learning are identified. Second, the extent to which transformative learning is *evidenced* in the EE is discussed. Third, the research method used within the study is outlined. Fourth, the case of Team Academy at a UK University is presented, and related findings are discussed. Finally, the implications that arise from the consideration of this case are discussed and suggestions for further research in this area are presented in the concluding comments.

Transformative learning

Since the development of Transformative Learning Theory some 40 years ago (Mezirow, 1978; Mezirow & Marsick, 1978), this emancipatory approach has drawn attention to the way in which as adults we can critically identify and challenge our own assumptions and beliefs (Cagney, 2014). Essentially a critical element of adult learning is about becoming cognizant of re-enacting our own lived experiences (Mezirow, 1978). Notions of transformation in this context are actually concerned with *perspective* transformation. That is, without meaningful shifts in the perspectives students have, transformative learning experiences are not possible. Central to the process of TL is the adult student interacting with problematic aspects of *their* life. An adult student is defined as an individual who is old enough to be held accountable for their own actions (Mezirow, 2000), something students of entrepreneurship in Higher Education primarily are. As noted recently (Jones, 2019), TL relates directly to EE through (1) its centrality to problem-solving and (2) the importance of problem-solving to entrepreneurs, and/or individuals capable of self-negotiated action. The problem-solving emphasis not being on a learned process, but rather a developed capacity to objectively reframe the assumptions of others and/or subjectively reframe one's own assumptions in order to arrive at transformative insight. Whilst TL can lead to more justified habits of mind, it also represents a journey for many that contains, grief, pain, and conflict (Cranton, 2016), given that it entails a fundamental de- and reconstruction of how an individual views themselves and their relationships (Mezirow, 1978). The nature of the process is outlined below (Table 1.1) with reference to Mezirow's (2000) ten stages through which such transformative insight is possible.

Table 1.1 Meizrow's (1991) 10 stages of transformative learning

---

1. A disorienting dilemma
2. Self-examination with feelings of fear, anger, guilt, or shame
3. A critical assessment of assumptions
4. Recognition that one's discontent and the process of transformation are shared
5. Exploration of options for new roles, relationships, and actions
6. Planning a course of action
7. Acquiring knowledge and skills for implementing one's plans
8. Provisional trying of new roles
9. Building competence and self-confidence in new roles and relationships
10. A reintegration into one's life on the basis of conditions dictated by one's new perspective

---

Source: Authors' own.

Cagney (2014) breaks these 10 down into four distinct parts that reconcile to a sequential learning process, these being (1) experience, (2) alienation, (3) reframing, and (4) reintegration. Through this process, students *experience* some form of a disorienting dilemma (as per Mezirow's stage 1). They then become *alienated* from prescribed social roles (as per Mezirow's stages 2–4). This leads to a *reframing* of one's conception of reality (as per Mezirow's stages 5–8). Finally, the student *reintegrates* back into society with a new perspective (as per Mezirow's stages 9–10). For Cagney, such an iterative process has the potential to enable students to restore balance to those moments in their lives where prior assumptions and beliefs are not aligned to the new experiences they encounter.

To summarize, TL is a process of education that is designed to facilitate the transformation of meaning perspectives in students (Mezirow, 1978). Whilst typically occurring within group settings, the process is focused on the transformation of individuals, specifically the psychological relations they hold with the inner and outer worlds (Jones, 2019). The stages of transformation can be viewed across 10 stages or through Cagney's (2014) distinct parts. Progression is seen as iterative (rather than linear), with stages often missed and/or repeated. The process is complex and must be driven by authentic experience of consequences in each individual student's life. The process of facilitating TL is also complex and taxing on educators. The following section will now consider the presence of TL in EE.

Transformative learning in entrepreneurship education

There is a long history of associating EE with transformational learning outcomes. For example, Ulrich and Cole (1987) noted the tendency to use pedagogies that supported active experimentation to support experiential learning outcomes. Pittaway and Cope (2007) acknowledge the importance of learning-by-doing and reflection, sometimes viewed as an alternative (Lourenco & Jones, 2006) to more traditional forms of business education. Acknowledgement that Mezirowian forms of experiential learning are embedded in EE is widely accepted (Arpiainen, Lackéus, Täks, & Tynjälä, 2013), although there is little agreement on how that might be so. There are clear examples of prescriptive agendas aimed at articulating how EE students can benefit through TL and what responsibilities, therefore, accrue to educators in the field. The recent work of Jones (2019) is proposing a (minimalist) signature pedagogy of EE places TL central to the foundations of all imaginable forms of EE, regardless of context. This work boldly highlights the issue of the types and nature of educator support for TL. In this respect, the EE literature does not speak explicitly as to the pedagogical demands on educators to facilitate TL. The work of Cranton (1994; 2016) has long been recognized as providing guidance around this issue.

To summarize, while clearly, an association between TL and EE has developed over time, exactly what constitutes TL in EE is not clear, especially from a Mezirowian perspective. Indeed, it would seem that Mezirowian TL, while often championed in the contemporary EE literature (Neck, Greene & Brush, 2014; Hägg, 2018; Jones, 2019), its implementation and effectiveness have been less considered. Given the educator factors noted above, it is timely to ask, is TL realistically possible in EE given the constraints often placed on educators in the domain of EE? This question shapes the remainder of the paper, starting with the research method used to explore this question. Then, an exploratory case study and related subsequently discussion provides the means to draw tentative conclusions as to the implications of embedding Mezirowian TL in EE.

Research method

An exploratory case study approach was chosen to enable an initial plausibility probe (Levy (2008) of the nature of TL in EE vis-à-vis educator approaches and student learning outcomes. The chosen method is considered ideal when detailed description of contextual events is required (Simons, 2014). Using triangulated data (Denzin, 1970) acquired from conversations with students and academic coaches employed to facilitate the Team Academy approach, the case data is presented as a reflection (see Becker & Renger, 2017) by one author on her role as coach, and then analyzed by both authors.

The case of Team Academy

In 1993 Johannes Partanen, at that time a marketing lecturer in the Jyväskylä University of Applied Sciences (JAMK), and frustrated with the approach taken to the delivery of his subject to HE students, decided to employ a new pedagogical approach. This approach has become globally known as Team Academy (or Tiimiakatemia). The Team Academy model requires learners to work in teams to set up and run real businesses or enterprises, where they have full ownership and control (Tosey, Dhaliwal, and Hassinen). Team Entrepreneurs (the term given to students on Team Academy programmes) engage in real-world trade-based activities.

The Team Academy model fosters risk-taking and freedom to create, developing entrepreneurial capacity through real rather than simulated experiences. The model creates a need to acquire knowledge and skills in order to develop business practice and ideas. Unlike traditional models of Higher Education delivery, the knowledge is not given or partially given by an expert (the lecturer or tutor). Instead, the coached approach catalyzes the TE to act in order to move forward. By its very nature, the coaching approach can (repeatedly) provide the disorienting dilemma Mezirow (1991) refers to. For some TEs this can prove extremely difficult and painful at times, and operating as a team can become tricky when there is an imbalance in those who have a natural desire to go and do, and those who don't:

"The biggest difference for me was about those who wanted to go and learn and develop, and those who didn't. That underpins nearly all of our function as a team" (student 1)[1].

When the team makes use of their individual skills and experience to support each other, often through the process of dialogue, but also frequently through informal means, their mindset begins to shift. The conversation below is typical of an exchange between TEs in a training session:

"For me, there has definitely been a switch in my mindset. I have become a totally positive person who sees the situation for what it is

and tries to work with it, when I used to be someone who just looks back and regrets. It came over a period of time of experiencing new things..." (student 2).

"What about in first year, I remember you saying you weren't as confident to put your ideas out but now you are. What made that change?" (student 3).

"I think it was definitely a confidence of doing new things. Starting to realize that I wanted to become better, I wanted to know more, do more. I found new passions and I think that brought out my confidence because I thought I know things I'm good at now" (student 2).

The transformative moments are not always earth-shattering and they don't always come directly after an incident that prompts transformation. Freedom to create and do is also an important part of the process, and it can create moments of rich learning that are not necessarily recognized immediately but come afterwards. Student 1 described the following:

"From an individual perspective, the most important thing for me has been developing a different thought process, which has happened through doing things. And then being able to reintegrate into a world outside of university – it's the new way of learning and wanting to develop that's had the most impact on me... that underpins all of my actions" (student 1).

And later, he continued:

"It's the individual's receptiveness to learning. You come into the programme thinking that you don't have to do anything you don't enjoy but integration into life as you go through the programme shows you that you have to do things in life that you don't enjoy. It's self-discipline and that filters down into the learning" (student 1).

For student 4 there was a similar change in mindset:

"Perspective for me is about what I would now do differently that I wouldn't do before. ... [for me there has been a] ... massive difference in the way that I want to do things. This course has changed my approach to what I do and how I do it. When I had an

experience of failure, it really made me stop and think 'what do I need to do differently...it made me go that extra step and my learning has improved so much from that" (student 4).

Developing connections with others and learning how to empathize in order to add value to an experience is something that also impacts the ability of TEs to create business opportunities for themselves and their teams. Student 4 explained his views on how his understanding of the importance of actually engaging with others openly has changed his experiences and his opportunities:

"It's even the little things ... I remember when I used to have a conversation with someone it used to be quite short because the other person would ask me 'how are you, what have you been up to?' and I would answer but I would never ask them 'what about you?' It sounds so simple, but I didn't used to think about that but now I do and I get a better connection with people".

For student 4, this was a transformational moment in his learning about the need to have connection and empathy with others, something that in the initial stages of his programme he struggled to understand or relate to. The freedom to choose learning, opportunities, and direction also means that the TEs have the freedom to choose not to be an entrepreneur. The language associated with entrepreneurship (entrepreneur, entrepreneurial, enterprising, etc.) can create challenges for individuals who view the concept purely as a venture creation discipline. The TEs on the BGU BTE programme explored what it was to be entrepreneurial and often defined that as taking risks, creating opportunities, learning from others, and enjoying what you do; for some that meant not going into business on their own:

"My perspective on all things has changed because of this course! I came in expecting to want to run a company when I hadn't really any idea what that meant. Now I know that this is definitely not what I want to do but I have learned to explore what I do want to do" (student 5).

The team construct creates many opportunities for transformative learning because of the shared dialogue and the shared jeopardy. What enables transformative learning to occur is complex to understand. Transformative learning requires the creation of moments of higher-order processing needed to ensure lasting change that requires students to frequently take stock of their experiences. Through this process, they construct practical and theoretical sessions for each other that support their growing knowledge base. The concept of a Team Academy as a community of practice is relevant here. Sharing a common goal with your team and team company creates a shared community of learning. Unlike in a more traditional programme where group work is not supported by a coached process or an understanding of team, this can create sticky or challenging moments (2002). In a Team Academy programme, the role of the team is to supportively challenge their colleagues in order to help them move forward through difficult situations. As student 1 put it:

"You get called out for not doing things. You can't bullshit and make up stuff and live in this la-la land ... well you can, but you won't develop into anything".

As part of the community, the coach is a fundamental component in the TEs' journey. Student 1 stated that for him the coaching was the most enabling element of the transformational learning journey. The coach comes to the process as an open participant in the journey, and, as far as is possible, the coach approaches the learning as an equal, even if they have greater knowledge and experience than the TEs in their team. The impact of this is eloquently stated by a TE when explaining the difference between the coached model and a traditional model of education delivery:

"The learning is boosted or enriched because I'm not waiting for you to come and tell me. Instead it's richer learning because if I go and do something, I want to come and tell you and my team rather than have you show me" (student 3).

The coaching approach challenges the TE in a supportive way that often leads to greater critical self-reflection and then changes in order to assimilate a new way of learning and being. The coach does not direct the change but rather offers up a mirror to the TE and, through effective and honest questioning, enables them to reframe what they see. As one TE stated:

"It enables me to fix things for myself, and for me that's what's at the heart of coaching; it's enabling. Enabling reflections on my actions" (student 6).

Connecting TL and EE

We are also to speak with confidence about the effectiveness of this coaching approach, vis-à-vis Mezirow's (1991) stages of transformative learning. By truncating Mezirow's ten stages into four distinct parts (see Cagney, 2014), a specific focus on (1) experience, (2) alienation, (3) reframing, and (4) reintegration emerges. Through this lens, the development of entrepreneurship students is evaluated in terms of the reconstruction of "meaning" perspective (Mezirow, 1978). The coached approach, coupled with the self-directed ethos of the Team Academy model, initiates a continual process of deconstructing and reframing meaning, both for the TEs and for the coaches. On the BGU programme, for the TEs arguably, the first experience of a disorienting dilemma arises as they meet each other for the first time. In fact, a TE's response to the question; 'have you experienced a disorienting dilemma in this model?' ... was to say:

> *"Yes! This course! I had to come to a university I hadn't been to, meet people I hadn't met before and then go away camping with them for two nights!" (student 9).*

The context for this meeting is a residential trip (known to them as Into the Woods) where the TEs are taken to camp overnight in a woodland for two nights. Into the Woods provides a form of challenging moment where the learners' assumptions are unpacked (Cagney, 2014), transforming the way they understand themselves and their place in the world of student-learner-entrepreneur.

Self-reflection, reflexivity, and self-awareness are key elements of the Team Academy model. From the start, therefore, the individual's understanding of who they are is challenged. Recognizing the possibilities of transformational change also highlights the possibilities for anxieties and discomfort to occur and this creates what Cagney (2014) from Mezirow (1991) has suggested is the alienation part of the phases of transformational learning. This sense of "not knowing" opens up the opportunity to explore previously untapped understanding and the positioning of oneself in relation to values and ideas. Moving from a state of surety to one of unknowing can reframe previously held beliefs. Student 7 describes the difference for them:

> *"It changes the approach I take with others ... when I speak with other people...you take the coaching home and you don't even know you're doing it. It's changing the way I think" (student 7).*

Reflexivity suggests an act or action; that of flexing, flexibility, the capacity to see around and beyond what is in front of you; a sense of turning or bending back to look forward (Vettraino, 2015). In the Team Academy model, the bending back or flexing takes place in a variety of ways, and often during the contact coached sessions – known as training or dialogue sessions. The key to the learning is that the knowledge gained is meaningful and lasting, although the action taken to "test out" a new role, relationship, or action will not necessarily be immediate:

> *"As someone who reflects later, I make a change following that and then I see that actually it's a better way of doing something or being" (student 7).*

Rather than the superficiality of the reflection referred to by Kemp (2001) as the "confessional narrative", the TEs experience of developing self-knowledge and reframing their understanding of their experiences is reflexive and felt, at times creating uncomfortable transformational paradigm shifts. For example, student 11 came into the Team Academy programme sure of his own sense of right and wrong, and his learning that there are an infinite number of shades of grey has led to a more productive approach to collaborative working for him:

> *"If I've made a mistake, I can accept that I am not always right, and the course is an excellent catalyst for this. You have to be very aware of other people in the team and conscious in dialogue of when you are assuming knowledge; there are lots of mature conversations! The learning I have taken is that the approach is very good for delivering a platform that enables you to say 'well, I might be right and I feel like I'm right but so is 'xxxx', and we both need to accept that things aren't always black or white" (student 11).*

In terms of TL relating directly to EE, three themes emerged. First the Team Academy model fosters risk-taking and freedom to create, developing entrepreneurial capacity through real rather than simulated experiences. Projects that the TEs undertake can generate substantial revenues, and potential losses as well. The Team Academy model fosters taking and managing risks, enabling the TEs to explore opportunities and ideas through real experiences; as students 10 and 9 observe:

"experience is a massive part of this process. This [approach] was a slap in the fact! It made me think 'this is real world and I better get on top of it!" (student 10).

The coach's role in this process is to challenge, question, and support the developing understanding from the knowledge the TEs seek out and acquire. As one TE put it:

"this teaches you about life" (student 9).

Second, the team construct creates greater opportunities for transformative learning because of the shared dialogue and the shared jeopardy. The process for dialogue is created through the coaching sessions that the team companies have each week. In these sessions, TEs explore problems and solutions predominantly related to their functioning as teams and their companies' performance. The conversation below is indicative of moments of learning that take place across time:

"It's like in our sessions, someone will say something in one session and then it'll come up in another session and we'll be like 'ahh! That's how it fits" (student 9).

"Yeah, like hunch theory … somebody has a hunch and it combines with another hunch and it all forms into one big idea, that's the connections between the sessions" (student 8).

"… and our discussions as well. Here we are encouraged to discuss and dialogue and that leads us to different ways of thinking" (student 10).

Third, the transformative moments are not always earth-shattering. Minor 'aha' moments that are instinctive and intuitive can come and go without being captured (Cunliffe, 2004; Corlett, 2012). Transformative moments are also not always immediate. What can move moments of learning from being insightful to being transformational, as noted by student 8 below, is the longevity of the impact, and the way in which the individual processes the transformative and/or pivotal moment:

"I reframe transformational learning as transformational development, transformational development is life and experience at the same time. You are not always aware of the learning or the change that happens, and I think that scenarios and situations in life that

impact on you, you're not always aware of until months down the line and you're in a similar situation and you respond differently to it. That's what this way of learning does" (student 8).

Discussion

What is clear on reflection is that the coach experiences the same process of experience, alienation, reframing, reintegration, particularly learning how to unlearn what we know or think we know about how students gain knowledge and understanding. This suggests that not only would it seem that the Team Academy approach is a very appropriate way to produce TL in EE, it may also serve as an excellent vehicle for developing scholarly practice as well. The ever-expanding role of EE requires more than mere knowledge and skill development; it also needs students to develop dispositions and human qualities that Barnett (2004) associates with performing an ontological turn. That is to say, how a student learns about themselves and their relations to all things external, will go a long way to ensure they are capable of navigating complexity, that Barnett claims is often radically unknowable.

Viewing the role of EE from this broader perspective, rather than strict business creation, highlights the potential for the Team Academy approach to support TL in EE. In this context, the emergent case findings contribute to the domain of enterprise/entrepreneurship education by demonstrating just *how* EE can be an important way of preparing students for the reality of an ever-changing world (QAA, 2018). In comparing the nature of the Team Academy approach to more traditional (although still experiential) approaches to EE, the development of student agency should not be assumed to be epiphenomenal vis-à-vis the engagement of students with enterprise curriculum. There are very specific student-, educator-, and institution-based factors that must align for transformational learning outcomes to be realized.

Reflecting further upon the case study findings, it is possible to imagine the advent of specialized EE programmes that are geared towards to development of students in preference to the development of ideas. At present, there is currently very little empirical evidence that a wide variety of EE programmes would satisfy the requirements of Mezirow's (1991) ten stages of TL. Put simply, there is typically too little runway to work with in terms of enabling students to adequately explore their own development alongside that of their ideas.

Conclusion

In conclusion, this initial plausibility probe into the effectiveness of the Team Academy approach to support TL in EE has produced promising results. Nevertheless, there is more to be done to establish the full potential of this approach in the domain of EE. We can further imagine several threshold levels under which TL outcomes should not automatically be assumed to occur. Our concern is not with those student outliers whose achievements can make ordinary teaching look very effective. Rather, our concern is with the conditions required at the level of the student cohort to support the possibility of TL outcomes. The nature of the student learning discussed in this paper shines light directly onto many potential constraints that may alienate educators and institutions from the Team Academy approach. However, it is unlikely the authentic benefits of TL will not come at a cost, for all involved.

Note

1 All student interviews referred to come from unpublished research carried out by Dr Elinor Vettraino.

References

Arpiainen, R., Lackéus, M., Täks, M. & Tynjälä, P. (2013). The sources and dynamics of emotions in entrepreneurship education learning process. *Trames*, *17*(4), pp. 331–346. DOI: 10.3176/tr.2013.4.02

Barnett, R. (2004). Learning for an unknown future. *Higher Education Research & Development*, *23*(3), pp. 247–260. DOI: 10.1080/0729436042 000235382

Becker, K. & Renger, R. (2017). Suggested guidelines for writing reflective case narratives: Structure and indicators. *American Journal of Evaluation*, *38*(1), pp. 138–150. DOI: 10.1177/1098214016664025

Cagney, A. (2014). Transformative learning. In D. Coghlan and M. Brydon-Miller (Eds.), *The SAGE encyclopedia of action research*. California: Sage Publications.

Corlett, S. (2012). Participant learning in and through research as reflexive dialogue: Being 'struck' and the effects of a recall. *Management Learning*, *44*(5), pp. 453–469. DOI: 10.1177/1350507612453429

Cranton, P. (2016). *Understanding and promoting transformative learning: A guide to theory and practice*. Virginia: Stylus Publishing.

Cox, R. (2017). *Assessing Transformative Learning: Toward a Unified Framework*. Available at: https://trace.tennessee.edu/utk_graddiss/4616, (accessed on 20/8/2019).

Cunliffe, A. (2002). Reflexive dialogical practice in management learning. *Management Learning*, *33*(1), pp. 35–61. DOI: 10.1177/1350507602331002

Cunliffe, A. (2004). On becoming a critically reflexive practitioner. *Journal of Management Education*, *28*(4), pp. 407–426. DOI: 10.1177/1052562904264440

Denzin, N. (1970). *The research act in sociology*. Chicago: Aldine.

Freire, P. (1974). *Pedagogy of the oppressed*. New York: Seabury Press.

Gibb, A. (1993). Enterprise culture and education: Understanding enterprise education and its links with small business, entrepreneurship and wider educational goals. *International Small Business Journal*, *11*, pp. 11–34. DOI: 10.1177/026624269301100301

Hägg, G. (2018). The reflective novice entrepreneur: From habitual action to intelligent action using experience-based pedagogy as a vehicle for change. In A. Fayolle (Ed.), *A research agenda for entrepreneurship education*, Cheltenham, UK and Northampton, MA, USA: Edward Elgar Publishing.

Hannon, P. (2005). Philosophies of enterprise and entrepreneurship education and challenges for Higher Education in the UK. *International Journal of Entrepreneurship and Innovation*, *6*(2), pp. 105–114. DOI: 10.5367/0000000053966876

Jones, C. (2007). Creating the reasonable adventurer: The co-evolution of student and learning environment. *Journal of Small Business and Enterprise Development*, *14*(2), pp. 228–240. DOI: 10.1108/14626000710746664

Jones, C. (2019). *How to teach entrepreneurship*. Cheltenham, UK and Northampton, MA, USA: Edward Elgar Publishing.

Kemp, M. (2001). Fictioning identities: A course on narrative and fictional approaches to educational practice. *Reflective Practice: International and Multidisciplinary Perspective*, *2*(3), pp. 345–355. DOI: 10.1080/1462394012 0103077

Levy, J. (2008). Case studies: Types, designs and logics of inference. *Conflict Management and Peace Science*, *25*(1), pp. 1–18. DOI: 10.1080/07388940701 860318

Lourenço, F. & Jones, O. (2006). Developing entrepreneurship education: Comparing traditional and alternative teaching approaches. *International Journal of Entrepreneurship Education*, *4*, pp. 111–140.

Mezirow, J. (1978). Perspective transformation. *Adult Education*, *28*(2), pp. 100–110. DOI: 10.1177/074171367802800202

Mezirow, J. (1991). *Transformative dimensions in adult learning*. San Francisco: Jossey-Bass.

Mezirow, J. (2000). *Learning as transformation: Critical perspectives on a theory in progress*. San Francisco: Jossey Bass.

Mezirow, J. (2008). An overview of transformative learning. In J. Crowther and P. Sutherland (Eds.), *Lifelong learning: Concepts and Contexts*. London: Routledge.

Mezirow, J. & Marsick, V. (1978). *Education for perspective transformation: Women's re-entry programs in community colleges*. New York: Columbia University Press.

Neck, H., Greene, P. & Brush, C. (2014). *Teaching entrepreneurship: A practice-based approach*, Cheltenham, UK and Northampton, MA, USA: Edward Elgar Publishing.

Pittaway, L. & Cope, J. (2007). Stimulating entrepreneurial learning: Integrating experiential and collaborative approaches to learning. *Management Learning*, *38*(2), pp. 211–233. DOI: 10.1177/1350507607075776

QAA (2018). Enterprise and entrepreneurship: Guidance for UK higher education providers, available at: http://www.qaa.ac.uk/en/Publications/Documents/Enterprise-and-entrpreneurship-education-2018.pdf (accessed September 14, 2019).

Simons, H. (2014). Case study research: In depth understanding in context. In P. Leavy (Ed.), *The Oxford handbook of qualitative research*. New York: Oxford University Press.

Taylor, E. W. (2007). An update of transformative learning theory: A critical review of the empirical research (1999-2005). *International Journal of Lifelong Education*, *26*, pp. 173–191. DOI: 10.1080/02601370701219475

Tosey, P., Dhaliwal, S., & Hassinen, J. (2015). The Finnish Team Academy model: Implications for management education. *Management Learning*, *46*(2), pp. 175–194. DOI: 10.1177/1350507613498334

Ulrich, T. & Cole, G. (1987). Toward more effective training of future entrepreneurs. *Journal of Small Business Management*, *25*(4), pp. 32–37.

Vettraino, E. (2015). Exploring the 6-part-story method as performative reflection: Reflections on embodied storytelling. In E. Vettraino and W. Linds (Eds.), *Playing in a house of mirrors: Applied theatre as reflective practice*. Rotterdam: Sense Publishing.

2 Programme Evolution, Success Factors, and Key Challenges

The Case of Team Entrepreneurship at UWE, Bristol

Berrbizne Urzelai and Lauren Davies

Introduction

Tiimiakatemia was developed in 1993 at Jyväskylä University of Applied Sciences (JAMK). In Team Academy (TA) students (known as *Team Entrepreneurs* or *TEs* in the UK) work in teams and learn-by-doing through running their own ventures (Tiimiakatemia, 2013). TA has been applied in different ways worldwide (Spain, Hungary, Romania, Tanzania, Mexico, Peru, etc.) but also within the UK (Northumbria, Bristol, Birmingham, Lincoln, etc.). As Tosey et al. (2015) point out, micro-cultures or local contexts in which pedagogical and cultural practices coalesce are not necessarily controllable or transferable, so TA models outside the host nation in Finland need to adapt considering elements such as social embeddedness, real-world application, identity formation, and normative attributes.

Along with Northumbria University, UWE Bristol was one of the first UK HE institutions to implement this programme back in 2013. Since then it has undergone significant development, including a major curriculum design change implemented in 2020, which includes the introduction of an enterprise and entrepreneurship competency framework.

In terms of the growth of the programme, Table 2.1 highlights that the number of students enroled has, for the most part, been increasing year by year, allowing the programme to run at full capacity with three new teams every year since 2015 (the exception was 2016 with two new teams). From 2013 until 2021 a total of 19 different team coaches have been involved in the programme, most of them being full-time members of staff at UWE.

In this chapter, we reflect on the evolution of the programme, and the experiences of the coaches, educators, and TEs that were involved in adapting and implementing the programme.

DOI: 10.4324/9781003163114-3

Table 2.1 Student enrolment

Year of entry	New Team Entrepreneurs	New teams
2013	27	2
2014	31	2
2015	45	3
2016	25	2
2017	44	3
2018	43	3
2019	47	3
2020	51	3
	313	**21**

Source: Authors' own.

In terms of methodology, our study could be considered action research as the authors are part of the organization within which the research and the change process were taking place (Eden & Huxham, 1996 and Coghlan & Brannick, 2005). We conducted seven semistructured interviews with Programme Leaders, Team Coaches, and TEs involved in the UWE TA programme. The interviewees were involved in it at different points in time from 2013 to 2020. The interviews were conducted in July and August 2020, just before the new programme design was implemented.

The key themes from the research are discussed in relation to the relevant theories identified within the literature review in terms of the curriculum design process, Entrepreneurship Education, and the pedagogies that have influenced this discipline.

We conclude with some reflections about how the programme has evolved, where it currently stands, and what its future could look like. The chapter contributes towards the identification of key success factors and challenges that educators face when implementing team-based, practice-led programmes, and how enterprise and entrepreneurship competence-based frameworks could be integrated into TA programme designs.

Curriculum design

Some of the questions we ask ourselves when designing an educational programme are related to the learning outcomes (*what do I want my students to know and to be able to do?*) or assessment (*what do I need to see to know they can do it? How can I get them to show me what they*

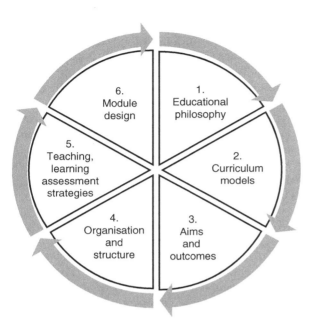

Figure 2.1 Curriculum design process.
Source: O'Neill (2015).

learnt?), but there are other elements that influence the way a programme might be designed and developed.

A six-stage curriculum design process is proposed by O'Neill (2015) as a framework on which to build new higher education programmes. This process considers not only the evaluation strategy but the context and the elements that define how to support students and staff (Figure 2.1).

The model suggests that the starting point for the design of a new programme should be to establish the educational philosophy, sometimes referred to as the *vision and values statement* to communicate the rationale of the programme. This should set out the programme's purpose(s), education and subject/discipline/professional values, the nature of the learning environment, and the key methods utilized for teaching, learning, and assessment, as well as the context in which the programme is operating.

The UWE Team Entrepreneurship programme was initially launched in 2013 when a group of educators from different disciplines within Bristol Business School became interested in the presentation delivered by Akatemia, a Community Interest Company focused on bringing the Finnish TA model to institutions in the UK, and decided to travel to Finland with other representatives of Northumbria University and University of Westminster to understand more. Then they split up into groups and visited other TAs such as those in Strasbourg, Mondragon, or Amsterdam.

> *"The teampreneurs[1] there surprised me as being what I'd expect from a young person on a good graduate development programme, in terms of their confidence, their level of experience, how they presented themselves, and how comfortable they were talking to external people"* (I1).

> *"In the initial programme team we all had a common interest in developing something that was a student-centred or/and enterprising in the University [...] I remember working on the mission, vision and values very well... we were like a group of TEs. You know grappling together, trying to figure out what we were doing and what was driving us. It wasn't just someone comes with something drafted and people say OK, this was painful"* (I2).

The interviewees' experience supports the model proposed by O'Neill (2015) in that the first step was identifying the educational philosophy. They worked together as a team to understand and design the programme's philosophy by looking at how TA was established in other countries. However, the reality is that the programme team did not follow a linear design process as such, and this was done in a more flexible way.

> *"The curriculum design process was iterative. I don't think we particularly looked at curriculum models. We started with the philosophy trying to get a deep understanding of the programme in Finland. We actually started from ethos, vision, mission, values. We had to adapt it to our microculture. What does that mean for the way that we deliver the programme?"* (I1)

At the start, the mission of the programme emphasized *revolutionising* Team Entrepreneurship, team learning and team leadership training and practice, *a new entrepreneur-led society,* and *nature and sustainable development*, suggesting the programme team were focused on how Team Entrepreneurship fitted into a broader picture in society.

"The values that we would instil within TE would actually go beyond TE and would kind of impact more widely in society…concepts of innovation and change and being brave and trying stuff and thinking about your impact and how you can be sustainable and how you can work with other people and make those connections. We really thought that we could kind of, you know, make a difference" (I2).

According to O'Neill (2015), the next stage should be to consider the curriculum models. Several authors in the field of curriculum design have referred to the dichotomy of the Product Model (Tyler, 1949) and the Process Model (Knight, 2001). The Product Model emphasizes plans and intentions (e.g. learning outcomes) and learning is largely controlled by the teacher, while the Process Model allows curricula to be designed in a more intuitive way with a greater level of student choice.

Based on these definitions, TA UWE mainly follows a process-based model as the learners engage in problem/enquiry-based activities that are personally relevant to them, including a negotiated curriculum and learner-centred design (e.g. learning contracts). The course not only focuses on the outcomes (e.g. venture creation/graduate career outcomes) but also on the process (personal development and team learning).

Interestingly, O'Neill (2015) classifies competency frameworks as product models, so the programme might have now moved to a middle point where the expectations and boundaries are defined but the learners have the freedom to *personalize* their learning and control how and when to develop those competences (for instance by deciding which workshops they want to attend or which projects they want to undertake).

"We've said that this programme is in the field of enterprise and entrepreneurship and therefore we should be able to have some expectations about what that means. […] philosophically, we are as process related as possible, but we have to create some kind of boundaries about what the scope of the programme is to be able to contain it" (I4).

"I like the idea of the new framework giving them a structure to start with. So, at year 1 having 'these are the clear things that you need to hit', but then by year 2 and 3 they start to define their own ways or things that they want to focus on more. We know that they have ticked the boxes, which gives them the grounding to be able to make

better decisions and have a better understanding of what it is that they want to do more. And then they start focusing on competencies that will help them to specialise in and push forward into a career in that space" (I6).

The third stage of the curriculum design process is to determine the programme aims and outcomes. Then the programme's organization and structure should be established, for example identifying the modules that the programme will comprise of and how these interlink. The fifth stage is to establish learning, teaching, and assessment strategies, which should align with the overall philosophy of the programme. The final stage is to design the individual modules within the programme, ensuring that they align with the philosophy, choice of curriculum models, aims and objectives, and the assessment strategies that have been established (O'Neill, 2015).

One of the challenges that the initial programme design team encountered was to achieve a balance between the institutional requirements and the innovative nature of the programme:

"There were always difficulties and challenges, largely because with the best intentions in the world, the Universities are bureaucratic systems. It's important for anybody working in an organisation to understand how the organisation works … so they could work within the bureaucracy … and still do what they wanted to do" (I3).

They also discussed the importance of aligning the programme design to the University strategy and finding key internal *champions*, particularly within the senior leadership of the university. Regarding teaching, learning, and assessment strategies, these needed to take into account the HE regulations and requirements. Besides, there were different views among the Team Coaches' team on where the focus should be:

"On the moment that you put business in the degree title you have a number of pieces of knowledge that any graduate with a business degree has to have. We ended up having to include some compulsory readings to make sure that we could say that our students had the basics around marketing, finance, etc. Our academic regs say that you must have at least 25% control conditions and controlled conditions were historically exams, so we had to figure out and what controlled conditions actually means to take exams out of the equation. Besides the coaching team is different in the UK as some of

us had experience running our own business but we were all academics and were also teaching on mainstream programmes" (I1).

"Some Team Coaches were kind of 'born again Team Academians' if you see what I mean? You know 'we mustn't divert from the true path which is Tiimiakatemia Finland' and at the other end of the spectrum people who were saying 'what's really important is that I give you information and knowledge and that you reference it properly using a Harvard system and that you are able to do proper academic work, as well as all this other practice stuff, which is kind of less important'….I'm exaggerating, but there was a divergence in views amongst the team" (I4).

The new UWE TA programme design launched in September 2020 (Figure 2.2) seeks to respond to the challenges and opportunities entrepreneurship educators face around the world to equip undergraduate students with entrepreneurial skills and develop their entrepreneurial mindsets and capabilities. The programme design has been informed by not only the Tiimiakatemia skill profile (Partanen, 2012), but the latest

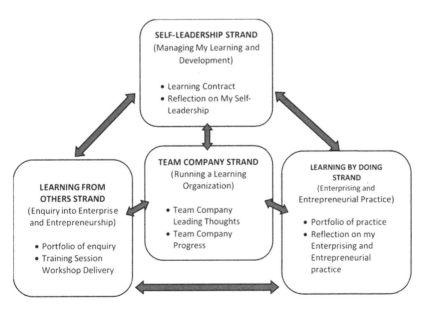

Figure 2.2 UWE Team Entrepreneurship strands.

Source: Authors' own.

advice from *UWE's Enterprise Skills Competency Framework* (UWE, 2020) the QAA's *"Enterprise and Entrepreneurship Education: Guidance for UK Higher Education Providers"* (Quality Assurance Agency (QAA), 2018) and the European Commission's *"EntreComp: The Entrepreneurship Competence Framework"* (Bacigalupo, 2016).

The programme is recognized as being at the forefront of developments in practice-led, self-managed, team-based enterprise and entrepreneurship education. The adoption of underpinning competency and enquiry frameworks allow the programme to maintain its position at the forefront of this evolving and developing discipline without requiring frequent revalidations of programme content. However, some interviewees seem to be curious (but still reluctant) about how the competence-based framework will work in practice:

> *"My personal view, based in industry is that there are no degrees of competence. You are either competent or you are not. I really don't understand how competence framework can translate into a University assessment"* (I3).

Entrepreneurship education and pedagogy

The term *entrepreneurial education* (EE) has been proposed as a unifying term for entrepreneurship education and enterprise education (Erkkilä, 2000) which takes into account the development of competencies needed to set up a venture, but also the idea of the student developing their self-reliance, self-insight, self-efficacy, creativity, initiative-taking and action orientation (Quality Assurance Agency QAA, 2018).

Approaches to entrepreneurship education were classified by Jamieson (1984) into three categories, with a fourth classification of *embedded* proposed by a number of authors including Gibb (2002).

1   *Teaching about:* Aimed at developing learners' theoretical understanding of entrepreneurship, guided by content.
2   *Teaching for:* A vocational approach to learn the skills, knowledge, and attitude needed to become an entrepreneur.
3   *Teaching through:* An experiential approach to develop an understanding of entrepreneurship through experiencing real entrepreneurial processes in 'safe' conditions.
4   *Embedded:* Entrepreneurship is delivered within non-business subjects with the aim of providing learners with entrepreneurial experience and awareness relevant to their field of study.

The Team Entrepreneurship programme can be seen as an example of a *Through* approach to Entrepreneurship Education (Jamieson, 1984; Berglund & Verduijn, 2018) whereby learners develop entrepreneurial skills, knowledge, and behaviours through real entrepreneurial experiences. However, there are debates about this, and about how this approach links to the new framework:

> *"I can see that the whole competency framework idea links very much into self-manage learning and vocational education and I think there are pros and cons to that... I think the program remains far too internally focused. I wouldn't call it learning by doing, I'd call it learning through doing. I don't think it has got that same sort of radical edge"* (I1).

The matrix in Figure 2.3 is a useful guide to considering the different approaches for teaching entrepreneurship today. As Neck et al. (2014) explain, the genesis is how entrepreneurship education was born, with a lack of theoretical underpinning. The apprentice cell takes a vocational perspective where skill development takes precedence over critical thinking and theory. The academic approach supports theory but at the expense of action (e.g. business plans as a dominant assessment

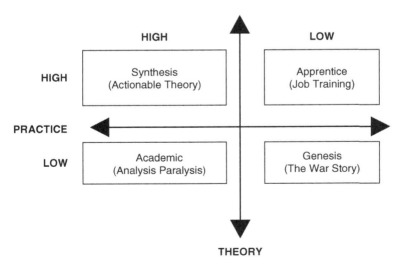

Figure 2.3 Theory-Practice matrix.
Source: Neck et al. (2014, p. 9).

method), while the synthesis cell provides the opportunity for informed application (where theory meets practice).

UWE TA takes the practice-based approach for *teaching* entrepreneurship (synthesis/actionable theory). In fact, the experiential element of the programme was highlighted by some interviewees as the most important element of the pedagogical model, but there were different views on how this was effectively implemented, or which resources the programme was providing.

> *"The experiential aspect of learning by doing for me felt like the biggest thing that was governing us [...] There was a lot more focus initially on doing projects (quick turnover projects that generated some quick cash). Doing and traveling. And experimentation {...} I think it went towards more reflection and less action. I think it was initially both"* (I2).

> *"The first year we made them [Team Companies] set up limited companies and we got a lot of pushback from that. There's been this gradual shift towards them becoming learning vehicles which is good in theory, but in practice it makes it's harder again to get the commitment to the team. That's part of what's behind the not going out enough and not doing customer visits, etc."* (I1).

The new programme design aims to strike a better balance between theory and practice and to be more inclusive in terms of what constitutes *learning by doing* and what it means to be enterprising and entrepreneurial.

> *"Previously TEs didn't get rewarded for being enterprising, because of the structure, which was to do with starting, growing and sustaining a venture. That didn't support those who were doing enterprising things, like leading a society for example. So, in terms of being practice led, I think the new model is more supportive of that"* (I6).

Neck and Corbett (2018) suggest a definition of EE as developing the mindset, skillset, and practice necessary for starting new ventures while recognising that the outcomes of such education are far-reaching, supporting the life skills necessary to live productive lives even if one does not start a business. They encourage a transition to teaching approaches based on adult learning.

Knowles et al. (2015) compared both andragogy and heutagogy and explain that adults need to know why they need to learn before engaging, they bring and analyze their own life experiences into their learning, they learn when they see application to real-life situations and their most potent motivators are internal (e.g. self-fulfilment) rather than extrinsic (e.g. better career prospects).

There are five major principles of andragogy-based teaching that are relevant to EE (Neck & Corbett, 2018), which state that the educator:

1   Exposes students to new possibilities of self-fulfillment.
2   Seeks to build relationships of mutual trust and helpfulness by encouraging cooperative activities and refraining from inducing [too much] competitiveness and judgement.
3   Helps students organize themselves (e.g. project groups) to share responsibility.
4   Helps students exploit their own experiences as resources for learning with discussions, role-playing, etc.
5   Helps students apply new learning to their experience to make the learning more meaningful and integrated.

Jones et al. (2019) argue that learning for enterprise and EE can be advanced through six knowledge bases (knowledge of self, of entrepreneurship theories, of transformational learning approaches, of authentic assessment processes, of student engagement, and of how-to scholarly lead) and that heutagogy must be evaluated alongside the blended contributions of pedagogy, andragogy, and academagogy.

Andragogy is often described as *self-directed* in nature but still anchored to the direction of the educator. Heutagogy is usually described as *self-determined* where student's interests and motivations create a focus area for new learning independent of the educator, so we could think of heutagogy as more *student-centred*. However, both imply that the student assumes a level of autonomy to drive their own learning.

The programme assumes, to some extent, that TEs come to it with a desire to learn about entrepreneurship because they are internally motivated to set up their own businesses and/or to develop enterprising skills and behaviours, and they learn when they see the application to real-life situations. However, they do not usually have a lot of life experience (mature students are quite rare within UWE TA) and many do not yet come with a clear idea on whether they want to become entrepreneurs, and they want to explore what that future path could look like for them while getting a university degree.

The educators in the programme define *what a TE means/ should be* by emphasizing attributes related to self-motivation, ambition, and future orientation.

"A teampreneur is a person, a learner who has their eyes open and who is awake. They really think about their learning, they think about who they are, they think about what they could do, what impact they could make in the world. When someone comes on the program, they might not be awake, but the programme wakes them up. In the first year we expected massive risk takers that were already awake" (I2).

"It's somebody who is managing their own learning in a team context who is grappling with and reaching conclusions about who they are and where they want to get to, to create their own futures and who are developing the ability to manage themselves, work with others and develop value" (I4).

They encourage learners to act as real entrepreneurs (the term *Team Entrepreneurs* rather than *students* is important), but some still exhibit what they consider a stereotypical student behaviour, e.g. lack of engagement, issues with attendance, and punctuality. Similar observations have been made in Northumbria when comparing engagement between Finnish and UK teams (Fowle & Jussila, 2016). This could reflect what Nielsen and Gartner (2017) identify as *multiple identities* in student entrepreneurship which they describe as a continuum from low (student or entrepreneur) to high (student and entrepreneur) identity plurality.

This related to some defining elements of the micro-culture in the UK, where TEs see themselves more as customers, they are at different places in their maturity cycle, or they are less comfortable with ambiguity:

"In Finland I think the fact that they don't pay fees is important [...] in the UK students regard themselves as customers, as investors. In Finland because you're being given your education, then you reciprocate by giving it your time and attention [...] Finnish students do two years of national service and tend to be a year older when they graduate... they are in a different place in the maturity cycle. Other academies have a much better gender balance than we have [...] and females tend to mature slightly earlier than males" (I1).

"In the UK we're not very comfortable with the 'happy clappy' side of TA. We don't do that very well. We're not very good at putting ourselves in a position where we are in the learning zone, we don't like being in the learning zone, we like being in the 'we know what we're doing zone'" (I5).

Student-centred and self-directed learning

Many terms have been linked with student-centred learning, such as flexible learning or self-directed learning, and therefore the term can mean different things to different people. Felder and Brent (1996) defined student-centred learning as a teaching approach that emphasises active learning over lectures and holds students responsible for their learning through self-paced and/or cooperative learning.

Gibbs (1995) describes student-centred courses as those that emphasize learner activity rather than passivity, students' experience not only on the course but outside and prior to the course, process, and competence rather than content, and learning decisions made by the student through negotiation with the educator.

One of the criticisms of traditional education is the reliance on teacher-centred methods of instruction that treat students as passive recipients rather than active participants. Self-directed learning plays an important role in adult learning theories (Candy, 1991) too. Grow (1991) identified four stages of self-directed learning, and Neck and Corbett (2018) used this model to map examples in Entrepreneurship Education (see Table 2.2).

Table 2.2 Stages of self-directed learning

Stage	Student	Teacher	Examples in EE
Stage 1	Dependent	Authority, coach	Interactive lectures, guest speakers, student pitching new ideas with immediate feedback, exams
Stage 2	Interested	Motivator, guide	Case studies, simulations
Stage 3	Involved	Facilitator	Feasibility projects, lean start-up, problem-based learning projects, design-thinking challenges, starting a business as a course project
Stage 4	Self-directed	Consultant, delegator	Starting a new venture outside of class or as part of independent study, students working on challenges facing a new or young venture (consulting project).

EE, entrepreneurship education.
Source: Neck and Corbett (2018, p. 16).

If we look at the role of the educator within the stages of self-directed learning, this could be related to the literature around coaching styles, that describe how the coach could adopt more of a push or pull style of coaching (Chartered Institute of Personnel and Development (CIPD), 2008), which influences their level of intervention and guidance. Within TA UWE we mainly adopt a facilitator's role. We also introduced the Mentors in Residence programme whereby business professionals mentor and provide .more directive guidance to our learners. Team coaching replaces traditional lectures to support a flexible learning approach (Blackwood et al., 2015).

Processes in TA are built on self-management where individuals take responsibility for their own learning and development and are empowered to experiment and learn from mistakes. They run their own training sessions, they work on their individual learning contracts and team's strategy to direct their learning activities towards their goals, they use group discussions, reflective diaries, and portfolios, and they manage their own time to run ventures and projects and bring the learning back to the team. However, as an interview argues, it is not just about that:

> *"I don't like the notion of self-managed or self-directed learning [...] this isn't what this programme is about (philosophy), it's so much more"* (I1).

Practice-led learning

Entrepreneurship is one of the most applied business disciplines where in order to *learn* entrepreneurship, you must *do* entrepreneurship. However, as Neck et al. (2014:9) argue, effective *doing* of entrepreneurship requires a set of *practices,* and these practices are firmly grounded in theory.

Approaching entrepreneurship as a method means teaching a way of thinking and acting built on a set of assumptions using a portfolio of practices to encourage creating, to go beyond knowing and talking actually into applying and acting (Neck et al., 2014). Some of its characteristics are summarized in Table 2.3 below.

Practices of entrepreneurship education include experimentation, play, empathy, creation, and reflection, which interlinks with each of the other practices (Neck et al., 2014). This relates to Kolb's (1984) notion of experiential learning as knowledge created through the transformation of experience, which focuses on the process of learning rather than on the outcomes. This is, what matters in the learning

Table 2.3 Method versus process

Entrepreneurship as a method	Entrepreneurship as a process
A set of practices	Known inputs and predicted outputs
Phases of learning	Steps to complete
Iterative	Linear
Creative	Predictive
Action focus	Planning focus
Investment for learning	Expected return
Collaborative	Competitive

Source: Adapted from Neck and Greene (2001), in Neck et al. (2014).

process is the experience, the feedback received, the interaction with others, and the reflection out of that process.

The new programme structure includes a new *Learning from Others* (LFO) strand that offers and sets up expectations around *knowledge, networking,* and *enquiry* to work towards the idea of *actionable theory.* This diverts from the original *venture, team,* and *individual* strands of the rocket model in Finland, and could be seen as linked to the basic subjects that some Team Academies (e.g. Mondragon) have.

> *"I sometimes worry about the balance in terms of whether or not we should be giving more input. Sometimes you know, having gone radical and said we are self-directed, self-managed, team-based, we don't have lectures, we learn by doing. Well, that's great, but I think that the pendulum could swing a bit. So, I thought it was a breakthrough when we decided to have the Learning from Others strand [...]other people have developed models, concepts, framework theories, and understanding those and being able to look at and testing and applying those can be useful, but that isn't the only learning from others that we do"* (I4).

In terms of the assessment strategies, the UK's higher education system influences the way that *theory* needs to be taught. Other TAs use the *book of books* as a reading list, but in UWE this evolved towards a more flexible framework of *research undertakings* with some core texts per module, and now that has evolved to a framework where TEs can engage in readings of their choosing, with some reading lists suggested. Interviewees argued that the *book of books* system was often too complex from an assessment viewpoint and it is suggested that the new framework aims to simplify the assessment strategy and *reward* those who are engaging in a wide range of activities.

Team learning

Although TA may appear at first sight to be informal and relatively unstructured, in fact, it has a highly developed pedagogy, but there is clearly a *TA way* of doing things that could at times conflict with UK culture and HE practices (Tosey et al., 2011).

Relatedly, while travelling to other Team Academies has been one of the fundamental elements in TA philosophy and many academies have learning journeys embedded in their curricula, this is not the case at UWE TA. The future of the programme may be around enhancing this international dimension or developing an online version of a team learning programme.

> *"Learning journeys are not a compulsory part of the course due to the UK legislation. If you are requiring them to pay for stuff you have to pay for it out of the fees (which will make the programme unappealing). Moving forward more attention needs to go into the internationalisation"* (I1).

> *"TE fits so well with the goals, mission, vision, and values of the university institution. As for the future as we get more and more into a virtual world, it's only becoming clearer how much people want connection and there's a reason why: you can get more stuff done in a team. More and more people are discovering it works and that it's not just... enterprise education. It's bigger than that. You know team learning"* (I2).

The theoretical base for TA's learning process comes from the organizational learning theories of Peter Senge (1990), and the knowledge creation theory of Nonaka and Takeuchi (1995) since TEs use team learning to share tacit and explicit knowledge within their team companies through dialogue sessions. Team learning is highlighted in the organizational learning approach. However, the way teams work in the UK is slightly different to Finland or other TA programmes due to the local context and culture. For instance, the TEs in Bristol are allowed to run individual projects and ventures, as long as they bring the knowledge back to the team.

"UK has a more individualistic culture than Finland or Spain. You have more work to do to build that sort of sense of collective accountability and responsibility [...] We never actually managed to make the TEs stick to the team targets... we removed because they weren't meaningful" (I1).

In terms of assessing team targets, this has been controversial, and many changes have been made since the programme first started. Interviewees reflected on the notion that there was no *penalty* if Team Companies did not meet targets and that this negated their usefulness as an assessment method. Team targets were removed but have now been re-introduced (i.e. targets about finance, reaching out through business proposals, and community engagement). This was as a result of the programme team having various discussions around the *team* element of the programme, and how having targets could set up explicit expectations and provide a strong driver to work as a team. The targets are linked to assessment more explicitly now and team-based assessments have a higher weighting in terms of credits within the new model.

Conclusions

The new programme design that UWE has adopted in 2020 might look different from the original Finnish model in terms of the learning processes (*strands* at UWE) but the principles are the same. The *individual, team company, and team* processes are present in our model (as *self-leadership, learning by doing* and *team company* strands) but we have explicitly added one more process: *learning from others* that links to the knowledge and community dimension of the programme (learning from research, readings, but also engagement with mentors, entrepreneurs, other team companies, other team academies, etc.), which somehow reflect the innovation and knowledge processes in TA. Customer and brand processes are embedded into the learning by doing strand, while leadership processes or team coaching elements of support processes are embedded within the team company strand.

The following Table 2.4 highlights the key success factors and challenges that have influenced the evolution of the UWE Team Entrepreneurship programme. Our findings show that curriculum design around TA programmes do not follow a linear process but establishing the ethos of the programme and having a strong and aligned team coaches' team has always been key. Being open and flexible to introduce changes and co-create the process with the TEs have also proved to be successful strategies for the implementation of any model. The new design

Table 2.4 Success factors and challenges in the UWE TE programme evolution

Success factors	Challenges
• A shared ethos and strong team coaches' team • Openness and flexibility in the implementation • Role model team entrepreneurs • A programme with experiential, team-based learning at its core • Co-creation with Team Entrepreneurs, listening to and responding to feedback • Clarifying the role of the coach (facilitator, assessor, mentor, etc.) • Strong international network and a well-established pedagogy established in Finland • Institutional support and resources • Strong network (mentors, businesses, team academies, etc.)	• Divergence in views between the programme team on what defines/distinguishes the programme • Achieving the right balance between theoretical and practice-based curricula • Defining the nature and scope of the team – balance between individual and team-based learning • Right balance between structure and freedom (requirements, competence development levels, etc.). • Not all learners act as "real" entrepreneurs – some reverting to stereotypical student mentality (multiple identities). • Cultural implications when applying TA pedagogy in UK context (individualism) • Resource intensive programme

Source: Authors' own.

stands in between process and product-based models and getting this balance right is one of the most challenging things for the programme team. Similarly, the dilemma between how to balance team-based and individual learning is an especially conflicting element due to a cultural influence. Programme reviews need to focus on the balance between structure and freedom, and requirements for the acquisition of competences in different levels and degrees for each year. The team also needs to recognise some of the success factors and elements that make the programme distinctive, such as the Mentors in Residence programme.

Reflecting on the key success factors and challenges that have shaped the evolution of the programme so far, what's next for UWE TA? The research conducted for this study and strategic discussions within the programme team have highlighted a few key areas for developing the programme further. The programme team have agreed a long-term vision to be a multi-programme TA and are beginning to explore how the TA pedagogy can be applied in other contexts outside of an undergraduate degree. This includes exploring options for joint international programmes with other Team Academies and exploring the application of the TA methodology not only within business and community settings but also in different disciplines. The diversity element of the programme is still to be developed (the cohort is predominantly *male*, *white*, *young*, and *home-based*) as this influences the learning opportunities and graduate outcomes, so diversity, internationalization, and a fully online delivery version of the programme are also on our radar for the future.

The programme team is continually evaluating the new programme design and will iterate and make further developments based on their own insights and feedback from TEs, thus continuing to emulate and the values of *learning by doing* and *co-creation* that have helped to define UWE Team Entrepreneurship.

Note

1 The learners in Team Academy programmes are usually named Team Entrepreneurs or Teampreneurs.

References

Bacigalupo, M., Kampylis, P., Punie, Y. & Van den Brande, L. (2016) *EntreComp: The entrepreneurship competence framework*. JRC Science for Policy Report. Luxembourg.

Berglund, K., & Verduijn, K. (2018). Introduction: Challenges for entrepreneurship education. In *Revitalizing Entrepreneurship Education* (pp. 3–24). Routledge. 10.4324/9781315447599.

Blackwood, T., Round, A., Pugalis, L., & Hatt, L. (2015). Making sense of learning: Insights from an experientially-based undergraduate entrepreneurship programme. *Industry and Higher Education*, 29(6), 445–457. 10.5367/ihe.2015.0278.

Candy, P. C. (1991). *Self-direction for lifelong learning. A comprehensive guide to theory and practice*. San Francisco, CA: Jossey-Bass. 10.1177/0741713692 04200307.

Chartered Institute of Personnel and Development (CIPD), (2008). *Coaching and buying coaching services*. https://www.portfolio-info.co.uk/files/file/ CIPD%20coaching_buying_services.pdf.

Coghlan, D. & Brannick, T. (2005). *Doing action research in your own organization* (2nd edn). London: Sage. 10.1080/09650792.2019.1692053.

Eden, C. & Huxham, C. (1996). Action research for management research. *British Journal of Management*, 7(1), pp. 75–86. 10.1111/j.1467-8551. 1996.tb00107.x.

40   *Berrbizne Urzelai and Lauren Davies*

Erkkilä, K. (2000). *Entrepreneurial education: Mapping the debates in the United States, the United Kingdom and Finland.* Abingdon, Taylor & Francis.

Felder, R. M., & Brent, R. (1996). Navigating the bumpy road to student-centered instruction. *College Teaching, 44*, pp. 43–47. 10.1080/87567555.1996.9933425

Fowle, M. & Jussila, N. (2016). The adoption of a Finnish learning model in the UK. *11th European Conference on Innovation and Entrepreneurship: ECIE 2016.*

Gartner, W. B. (1990). What are we talking about when we talk about entrepreneurship? *Journal of Business Venturing, 5*(1), pp. 15–28. 10.1016/0883-9026(90)90023-M.

Gibb, A. (2002). In pursuit of a new enterprise and entrepreneurship paradigm for learning: creative destruction, new values, new ways of doing things and new combinations of knowledge. *International Journal of Management Reviews, 4*(3), pp. 213–232. 10.1111/1468-2370.00086.

Gibbs, G. (1995). *Assessing student centred courses.* Oxford: Oxford Centre for Staff Learning and Development.

Grow, G. O. (1991). Teaching learners to be self-directed. *Adult Education Quarterly, 41*(3), pp. 125–149. 10.1177/0001848191041003001.

Hannon, P. (2005). Philosophies of enterprise and entrepreneurship education and challenges for higher education in the UK. *The International Journal of Entrepreneurship and Innovation, 6*(2), pp. 105–114. 10.5367/0000000053966876.

Jamieson I (1984) *Schools and enterprise.* In: Watts A.G. and Moran P. (eds). *Education for Enterprise.* Cambridge: CRAC, pp. 19–27.

Jones, C., Penaluna, K., & Penaluna, A. (2019). The promise of andragogy, heutagogy and academagogy to enterprise and entrepreneurship education pedagogy. *Education+ Training, 61*(9), pp. 1170–1186.

Knight, P.T. (2001). Complexity and curriculum: A process approach to curriculum making. *Teaching in Higher Education, 6*(3), pp. 369–381. 10.1080/13562510120061223.

Knowles, M. S., Holton, E. F. III, & Swanson, R. A. (2015). *The adult learner: The definitive classic in adult education and human resource development* (8th ed.). New York, NY: Routledge. 10.4324/9780080481913.

Neck, H., & Corbett, A. (2018). The scholarship of teaching and learning entrepreneurship. *Entrepreneurship Education and Pedagogy, 1*, pp. 8–41. 10.1177/2515127417737286.

Neck, H.M., Greene, P.G. & Brush, C.G. (2014). *Teaching entrepreneurship: a practice-based approach*, Cheltenham, UK: Edward Elgar.

Nielsen, S. L., & Gartner, W. B. (2017). Am I a student and/or entrepreneur? Multiple identities in student entrepreneurship. *Education+ Training, 59*(2), pp. 135–154. 10.1108/ET-09-2014-0122.

Nonaka, I., & Takeuchi H. (1995). *The knowledge creating company: How Japanese companies create the dynamics of innovation.* Oxford: Oxford University Press.

O'Neill, G. (2015). *Curriculum design in higher education: Theory to practice.* Dublin: UCD Teaching & Learning. ISBN 9781905254989. http://www.ucd. ie/t4cms/UCDTLP0068.pdf.

Partanen, J. (2012). *The Team Coach's Best Tools.* Jyväskylä: Kopijyvä Oy.

Quality Assurance Agency (QAA) (2018) *Enterprise and entrepreneurship education: Guidance for UK higher education providers.* Gloucester, UK: The Quality Assurance Agency for Higher Education. https://www.qaa.ac. uk/docs/qaas/enhancement-and-development/enterprise-and-entrpreneurship-education-2018.pdf?sfvrsn=15f1f981_8.

Senge, P. (1990). *Fifth Discipline: The art and practice of the learning organization,* Century.

Tiimiakatemia (2013). *Tiimiakatemia in a nutshell.* [Online] Available from: http://www.tiimiakatemia.fi/en/tiimiakatemia/tiimiakatemia-nutshell/ [Accessed 1st July 2017].

Tiimiakatemia Global, (2016). *Leading thoughts.* [Online] Available from: http:// tiimiakatemia.com/en/company/leading-thoughts [Accessed 01 July 2017]

Tosey, D., Robinson, D., Biggs, N. & Dhaliwal, D. (2011) *CHAPTER C4 Exploration of the feasibility of the Finnish 'TA' approach as an innovation within a UK business education context.* Guildford: University of Surrey.

Tosey, P., Dhaliwal, S., & Hassinen, J. (2015). The Finnish TA model: implications for management education. *Management Learning, 46*(2), pp. 175–194. 10.1177/1350507613498334.

Tyler, R.W. (1949). *Basic principles of curriculum and instruction.* Chicago: University of Chicago Press. 10.7208/chicago/9780226820323.001.0001.

University of the West of England (UWE) (2020). *Enterprise skills competency framework.* https://intranet.uwe.ac.uk/tasks-guides/Guide/embedding-enterprise-in-the-curriculum.

3 HES-SO Business Team Academy

How to Evaluate Without Exams?

Antoine Perruchoud and Lionel Emery

Introduction

The HES-SO Team Academy is part of the Business Administration Bachelor. Launched in 2017, this unique programme in Switzerland is inspired by the Finnish *Tiimiakatemia* methodology developed by Johannes Partanen. Teampreneurs (Team Academy students) carry out real projects for companies or develop their own projects. The students of our programme (hereafter teampreneurs) have 3 years to develop 21 competences:

- The first year is devoted to a kind of *unlearning* of pedagogical models they have usually practiced so far (success mainly based on individual exams by subjects). As teampreneurs they learn to be autonomous and must acquire essential skills on different topics. It is also during this phase that they devise an individual learning contract and team objectives. However, rather than *unlearning* we should talk about *hyperlearning*, discovering a way of learning beyond known models!
- In the second year, teampreneurs develop more specific skills and become very independent. They consolidate a key attitude discovered in the first year: Success depends on daily contact between the local socio-economic system and potential customers. Their self-organized learning accelerates.
- In the last year, each teampreneur is at ease in the development and implementation of projects as well as building and managing customer relationships. They are now aiming for innovation and entrepreneurial action!

Description of the structure of the assessment process

Within the study programme Team Academy from the HES-SO, promotions take place annually in the first year, then each semester for

DOI: 10.4324/9781003163114-4

the second and third years. Semesters 1–6[1] each contain 2 modules. The 6th semester includes, in addition, a module for the bachelor's thesis. Promotions for semesters 1–5 are based on 2 main modules per semester:

- the *learning path* module must reflect/measure the quantity and type of actions carried out by the teampreneur during a semester.
- the *portfolio of competences* module must reflect/demonstrate the teampreneur's level on each of the 21 competences covered by the Business Team Academy programme.

1   Learning path:
Each teampreneur is responsible for documenting his or her journey through a personal learning journal or portfolio. This *learning path* module contains 5 parts per semester, as well as an additional element (learning journey) for semesters 2, 4, and 5. This module is divided as follows:

Active participation

- Dialogue Sessions (DS): Twice a week, all team members and their team coach meet for two to four hours to discuss and exchange with each other. The topics of the sessions can be used both to exchange knowledge and experience as well as to define objectives and the organization/functioning of the team.
- Training Sessions (TS): In cooperation with the team coach, the team members plan and organize the training sessions during the semester as a team. For each of the training sessions, an expert and specific topic are chosen (for example digital marketing, team leadership, etc.), and learning objectives to be achieved in teams are set.
- Learning Journeys (LJ): During semesters 2, 4, and 5, teampreneurs must organize and participate in a trip/exchange within the Team Academy's international network, or possibly in another entrepreneurial and learning context.

Proof of learning

- Applied Projects (AP): Teampreneurs must carry out projects in teams (at least 3 people) and get in touch with the market and real customers. For each project, a qualitative and quantitative follow-up of the results obtained is established and made available to all teampreneurs and the team coach.

- Individual Readings (IR): In accordance with the themes addressed in the dialogue sessions or training sessions, or following the problems encountered in the realization of projects for the Team Company, each teampreneur undertakes readings to regularly increase his or her level of knowledge and to transmit the content of his or her learnings to his or her team (directly in DS or through a form of *booktubing*).

- Reflective Articles (RA): This individual document shows the scope of the learning achieved by the teampreneur through different training sessions, individual readings, projects, coaching sessions, and learning journeys. It is also for the teampreneur to develop a constructive and critical posture on the development of his or her skills, in an organized and structured written form.

The teampreneur accumulates validated points from his/her participation and contributions to dialogue sessions, training sessions, or learning journeys. In the same way for the individual readings, the writing of reflective articles, and carrying out applied projects, several points are awarded to the teampreneur according to pre-established criteria for each validated activity.

For each semester, a minimum number of points is set and, on this basis ECTS (European Credits Transfer Scale) credits related to this module are acquired or not. For this *learning path* module, each semester, teampreneurs must demonstrate via their individual learning portfolio, the acquisition of at least 100 points. The distribution of points requested for each part (DS, TS, IR, etc.) of the module may vary from semester to semester. The points are validated twice a year via a 360° evaluation. Please refer to appendix 1 for the detail of the points required to validate each part of the *learning path*.

Regarding this *learning path* module, the quantitative objectives set for each semester have proven to be very demanding and require the learner to quickly develop a strong capacity for self-management. Most of the remediation that we have had are due to *project hours* or *insufficient number* of validated readings or reflective articles at the end of the semester.

Figure 3.1 below shows that Andromeda Cooperative (the first team company in the programme) as a team has always managed to exceed the minimum number of project hours set by the programme (e.g. at least 200 validated hours per teampreneur for semester 1). *Learning by doing* works and it is sometimes necessary to put the brakes on some teampreneurs who are much more on a *doing by doing*.

Our learning model, based on the Kolb cycle (see Figure 3.2) has proven to be very effective: action–theory–reflexivity – experimentation

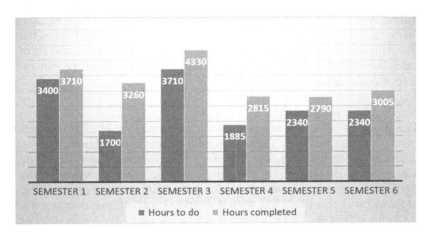

Figure 3.1 Comparison between project hours to do and project hours completed (Andromeda).

Source: Perruchoud and Emery (2020).

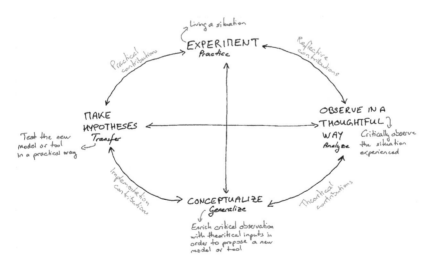

Figure 3.2 Adapted from Kolb's learning cycle.

Source: Kolb (2015).

(Kolb, 2015). Reading and writing articles is perceived as a major constraint, even a shock at the beginning of the programme. But very quickly, thanks to the weekly dialogue sessions and the demonstration effect of the first deliverables and their impact team learning is set up and the team coach ensures that everyone regularly delivers these theoretical and reflective contributions.

2 Portfolio of competences:

The *portfolio of competences* module is based on 21 competences covered by the Business Team Academy programme (Figure 3.3).

These 21 skills were adapted for *Tiimiakatemia* and Ecole de Management de Strasbourg. We have modified them according to the feedback we received from representatives of different organizations in order to bring them into line with the expectations of Swiss employers.

Of these 21 skills, 14 are so-called *hard skills* and 7 are social skills or *soft skills*. The development of non-technical competences is quite unique in a university-level degree in Switzerland. These skills are now very much in demand among recruiters and therefore bring great added value to our students on the job market. For each of the skills, a level of development ranging from *beginner 1* to *professional* has been established. Figure 3.4 is, as an example, a description of the *leadership* competence.

The principle of competence development is as follows:

- Beginner 1: expression of a situation
- Beginner 2: theoretical knowledge of the competence
- Advanced practitioner 1: has practiced the skill at least once with

Learnig in Team
1. Information processing and ICT skills
2. Team learning
3. Method and personal attitude to learn to learn
4. Creativity and innovation
5. Communication in English and German
6. Interpersonal communication
7. Autoinitiative

Team leader
8. Self-management and self-discipline
9. Project management
10. Team leadership
11. Economy and society
12. Coaching and skills development
13. Business strategy
14. Self-leadership

Team Entrepreneur
15. Customer relations, negociation and sales
16. Corporate finance
17. Marketing
18. Statistics anddatamanagement
19. Culture and international developpement
20. Network creation
21. Enrepreneurial actions

Figure 3.3 21 competences targeted.

Source: Perruchoud, Emery, Rey, Cavin (2020a).

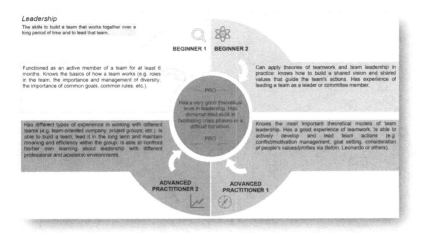

Figure 3.4 Example of the *leadership* competence.

Source: Perruchoud, Emery, Rey, Cavin (2020a).

> the contribution of theoretical elements, the action is done consciously
> • Advanced practitioner 2: has practiced the competence several times and in several contexts using various theoretical sources
> • Professional: is able to take the role of a mentor

For this module, each semester, the teampreneur must demonstrate through his or her portfolio the progress made (or not) for each of the 21 competences and thus obtain (or not) a minimum number of points previously defined according to a grid (refer to Appendix 1 for the detail of the points required to validate *the portfolio of competences*).

At the end of the semester, each teampreneur is responsible for collecting all the necessary information and evidence in a single document or on a personal website. The publication of this portfolio and the sharing of it with peers and the jury is the key moment of the completion of each semester.

A significant challenge for our Business Team Academy is the choice of a digital platform which allows the co-construction, traceability, mapping, and sharing (Figure 3.5 below) of knowledge and projects both in a team vision and in the individual monitoring of each teampreneur's portfolio.

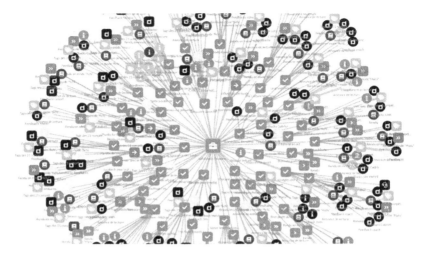

Figure 3.5 Automated mapping of learning portfolios over 1 semester via our platform hazu.teamacademy.ch.

Source: Perruchoud, Emery, Rey, Cavin (2020b).

Thanks to this portfolio and the 360° evaluation (explained hereafter) we have the possibility to assess the impact of the activities undertaken for the acquisition of these skills and to recognize the teampreneur's level of progress on a scale: beginner 1 - beginner 2 - advanced practitioner 1 - advanced practitioner 2 - professional. The establishment of this 360° is done through self-evaluation, peer evaluation, and final validation by coaches and an external expert.

Description of the assessment process

During the semester the teampreneurs carry out projects, present readings, publish articles, etc. Each activity is subject to feedback by at least one teampreneur and validated by the team coach.

At the end of the semester, they must deliver two documents. The first is a dashboard that summarizes all activities and actions carried out during the half-year. The academic staff validates the dashboard and each teampreneur is awarded the relevant points.

The second one is an individual portfolio that each teampreneur has to complete. The format of the portfolio is free, but it must at least contain:

1 An introduction and key numbers;
2 The actual individual learning contract;
3 A summary of main activities (readings, project hours, reflective articles, etc.);
4 A demonstration of the skills developed (self-assessment of the 21 competences).

For the 360° evaluation, groups of 4–5 teampreneurs are formed and each day is dedicated to the evaluation of one group of teampreneurs.

The first part of the day is dedicated to the presentation of the portfolio to the other teampreneurs and the jury. The jury is formed by four persons:

- The team coach who has the global view of the actions made by each teampreneur;
- The head coach who has the global view of all teampreneurs;
- The academic collaborator who is responsible for the evaluation process and the fair treatment of each teampreneur;
- An external expert (an entrepreneur, a CEO, a HR manager, ...) who represents the professional community (employers) and their practices.

During the second part of the morning, the teampreneurs evaluate each other's skill levels and give each other constructive feedback on the development of their 21 skills. Following this, each teampreneur can review his or her own self-evaluation.

In the afternoon, each teampreneur meets with the jury. The purpose of this moment is twofold. Firstly, it is to take stock of situations over the semester by highlighting the teampreneur's level of progress on the 21 competences targeted by the programme. Secondly, the coaches guide the teampreneurs on the learning path to be taken during the following semester, in order to give him or her elements to write his or her new learning contract for the next semester.

At the end of this process, several documents are sent to the teampreneur. The first one is the formal evaluation protocol which contains the level achieved on each competence. The other two are written feedback and general observations from the coaches and the external expert.

Analysis of the evaluation process

Since 2017, we have carried out six 360° evaluations (1 per semester) for all teampreneurs. This represents 175 individual assessments according to the methodology described above.

After each 360° evaluation session, a questionnaire is sent to all teampreneurs. A section of this questionnaire is dedicated to the evaluation process. In total, we obtained 128 responses over 3 years, i.e. an average response rate of 73.15%. Below are some of the key elements taken from these questionnaires concerning the evaluations.

Level of satisfaction with the evaluation process

Out of all the answers obtained, no teampreneur is at all dissatisfied with the overall evaluation process. 31.25% say they are moderately satisfied and 68.75% are satisfied or very satisfied with the way the evaluations are carried out (Figure 3.6).

Level of usefulness of the assessment process

86.4% of students find the different parts of the evaluation process useful or very useful. The most useful part is the individual interviews with the jury (95.29%). This is followed by written feedback from experts (90.75%) and coaches (87.50%) and the evaluation protocols (86.32%). The peer review is the part that students find least useful, with 78.63% of students rating this part as *useful* or *very useful*, which is still a very good score (Figure 3.7).

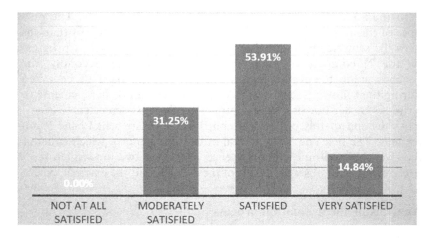

Figure 3.6 Level of satisfaction with the evaluation process.
Source: Emery (2020).

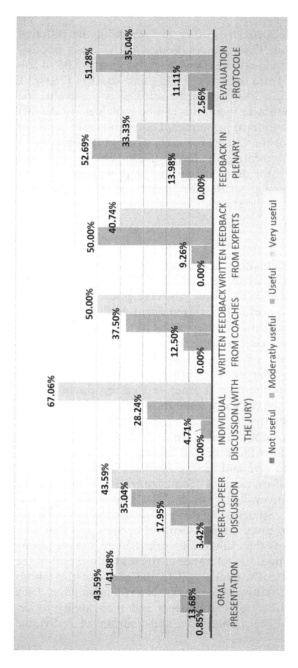

Figure 3.7 Level of usefulness of the parts of the evaluation.

Source: Emery (2020).

Level of satisfaction of the assessment process

74.75% of students are *satisfied* or *very satisfied* with the different stages of the evaluation. Oral presentations are the most popular (85.71%). Then, the individual interviews with the jury (78.05%) followed by the feedback from experts (78.13%) and coaches (75.00%). The element with which students are least satisfied is the evaluation protocol. After discussion with them, this can be explained by the fact that the students expect to have personalized comments and areas for improvement for each of the 21 competences, whereas the aim of this document is limited to indicating the levels of competences validated for each semester. Paths for development and improvement are conveyed to the students through written feedback from the coaches or in a one-on-one interview at the students' request Figure 3.8.

Qualitative feedback

Students report that evaluations are important moments for them. They provide an opportunity to acknowledge all the work they have done during the semester so that they can take pride in their work. Students also note the importance of this moment in raising awareness of their strengths and potential for development.

Critical feedback from coaches, external experts, and peers is appreciated and is a source of development for the coming semester. Some teampreneurs describe the 360° evaluation as a difficult moment to live through because of the stress it generates and because of the fact that the self-perception of the work done during the semester is very different from the work effectively done by the teampreneur.

All the teampreneurs emphasize that this new method of evaluation is difficult to understand without having experienced it at least once. They must learn how to give and receive feedback as well as how to evaluate themselves (self-evaluation). The change of role of the team coach who becomes an evaluator during the evaluation period is sometimes questioned. Students appreciate that coaches open up moments of dialogue to discuss the assessment process and that coaches remind them of how the evaluation works before it takes place.

Our external experts note the relevance of the evaluation grid of the 21 competences, which corresponds well to the needs of the labour market. The mix of soft skills and hard skills is a real advantage. They also point out the maturity of the students and their ability to demonstrate their skills. The publication and sharing of individual

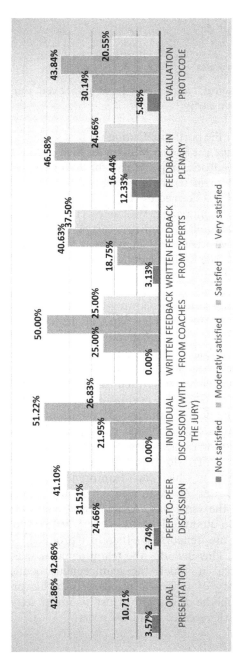

Figure 3.8 Level of satisfaction of the parts of the evaluation.

Source: Emery (2020).

learning portfolios allow them to get to know the students before meeting them on their assessment day.

Improvement of the evaluation process

Based on all the elements presented above, we have improved our evaluation process in the following way:

- The testing of several tools for the portfolio. During the first semester, we required teampreneurs to use the Switch Mahara for the portfolio. We received much negative feedback. In particular, this tool gave the teampreneurs too little freedom in terms of personalization of the portfolio, and as well the tool was deemed too complicated to use. In the 2nd year, we provided the teampreneurs with an excel template in which the teampreneur indicated all the activities carried out during the semester (readings, reflective articles, training sessions, etc.) as well as the demonstration of skills. The feedback obtained by the students was not very satisfactory because the excel template was too quantitative and limited the qualitative elements (in particular the learning achieved by the teampreneurs). Following this feedback, we no longer imposed the form of the portfolio. Most of the students produce a portfolio in word or pdf format and a minority use computer platforms such as websites. This alternative allows teampreneurs to take ownership of their portfolio and create a personalized version that highlights the creativity of each teampreneur.
- One of the most sensitive parts of the evaluations is the peer-evaluation. This is because students evaluate each other, and it is important that the evaluations and feedback given are fair and objective. We have sought to avoid bias in these peer-assessments (over- and under-evaluation). To do this, we created a peer-evaluation grid of competences in which each teampreneur had to explicitly evaluate each of the 21 competences of the other teampreneurs evaluated on the same day. After several tests, we realized that this grid was too quantitative and left very little room for discussion between the teampreneurs. We therefore produced a second version of this grid. This includes the teampreneur's self-evaluation, a comment area in which the teampreneur being assessed provides a summary of feedback received from his or her peers and an area in which he or she can adjust his initial self-evaluation following feedback received from his peers.

- The third important adaptation we have made to the evaluation process is the delivery of different documents to students. These are:

  - Written feedback from the external expert
  - Written feedback from programme coaches
  - Protocol for evaluating and validating the skill levels

These documents enable students to keep a formal written record of the items discussed during the assessment. In addition, they allow them to concentrate fully on their assessments without worrying about taking notes.

- The clarification of the different roles has also been an important element of improvement. Indeed, the team coach who supports, coaches, and seeks to develop the teampreneurs' skills throughout the semester must, during the evaluations, change his or her role in order to be an evaluator. In addition, the role of each member of the jury must be clearly explained to the students so that they understand each other's roles. This will also avoid frustration following the assessments.
- Following the various feedbacks we received from external experts and different socio-economic circles, we have adjusted the 21 competences in the following manner:

  - Specifying certain soft skills such as *self-leadership* and *entrepreneurial action*;
  - Explicitly introducing language objectives in German and English;
  - Bringing together creativity and innovation;
  - Adding the *economy and society* competence.

Employers' views on the evaluation system

The first graduates of the HES-SO Team Academy received their diplomas in September 2020. They began their training in 2017 in a class of 17 teampreneurs. We had 4 failures and 7 dropouts. The reasons for these are twofold: some teampreneurs find it difficult to be self-motivated and work as part of a team while others realize that this pedagogical model does not fit with them.

Of the 17 teampreneurs who started their training in September 2017, 11 obtained their bachelor's degrees. Of these 11 alumni to date, we have 5 entrepreneurs (project developed in the Team Academy or other), 3 employees (working for someone else), 2 graduates managing various mandates, and 1 looking for a job.

Employers welcomed the new graduates of the HES-SO Team Academy very favourably. This shows, on the one hand, that the work carried out by the teampreneurs to develop their skills is consistent and, on the other hand, that the 360° evaluation system put in place makes it possible to recognize the levels of skills achieved by the students.

One of the employers of an alumni said, *"When he gets involved in a project, he invests himself thoroughly and always pushes the thinking further than I ask him to. He quickly became my right-hand man".* When this employer talks about the Team Academy's evaluation system, he says, *"Through the Team Academy's evaluation system, the student has to convince his peers and coaches that he is competent in a range of areas. This is far more valuable than marks".*

Conclusions

It should be noted that the Team Academy's 21 competences framework contains both *hard skills* and *soft skills*. According to feedback from our external experts, this is a real added value of the Team Academy programme.

The 360° evaluation system in place requires a significant investment of time but is necessary to guarantee the quality of the training: a full day to evaluate a group of 4–5 teampreneurs. The systematic inclusion of an external expert/a representative of the local socio-economic environment is also a key factor in the success of our assessment process. Feedback from those external experts are very much appreciated by our teampreneurs but are also an important source of continuous improvement.

However, we note the difficulty for students, particularly in the first year, to understand the purpose of the self-evaluation and the differentiated role that coaches adopt, who, in the context of an evaluation, are more critical.

The evaluation protocols drawn up by the jury are sent to the teampreneurs and to the academic administration of the school in charge of delivering the corresponding ECTS. They formally establish the success or failure of the two modules: (1) the learning path and (2) the portfolio of competences. Cases of remediation concerned both shortcomings in the *pathway* and failures in the *portfolio* to demonstrate the competences acquired during the semester.

Considering the results of the skill levels achieved by the teampreneurs at the end of their training, we note that – in general – the level of the students who have followed the Business Team Academy programme corresponds to the requirements expected by the market: young people who are employable, responsible, and autonomous.

Based on our experience, feedback from the professional community, and from our first alumni, we are confident that our Business Team Academy offers a new training path that complements the existing offer of Business Administration courses at HES-SO. In addition, it provides young graduates to the job market who have benefited from a solid first practical experience and a level of competences in both *hard skills* and *soft skills* such as self-management, self-leadership, learning to learn, creativity, interpersonal communication, entrepreneurial action, or team leadership.

These first *Team Academy* graduates in Switzerland are therefore rather well equipped to manage their emotions in today's uncertain and chaotic situations. Moreover, the team learning process they experienced for 3 years has definitively anchored them in approaches that are very often *theorized* but not very practical: collective intelligence and caring leadership!

Note

1 Semesters 1, 3, and 5 run from mid-September to the end of January, and semesters 2, 4, and 6 run from mid-February to the end of June.

References

Emery, L. (2020). *Team academy teampreneurs' satisfaction survey* 2017– 2020.
Kolb, D.A. (2015). *Experiential learning*. Upper Saddle River, New Jersey: Pearson Education.
Partanen, J. (2019). *The team coach's best tools*. Jyväskylä: Grano Oy.
Perruchoud, A., Emery, L., Rey, J.-C., & Cavin P. (2020a). *Team Academy Notebook 2020*.
Perruchoud, A., Emery, L., Rey, J.-C., & Cavin P. (2020b). *Hazu*
Perruchoud, A., & Emery, L. (2020). *Team Academy report* 2017–2020.

Appendices

1   Evaluation of lthe *learning path* module (1st year):
The teampreneur must obtain at least 100 points on this module per semester, with at least the points indicated under *minimum* in the following Table 3.1:

2 Evaluation of the *portfolio of competencies* module (1st year):
The teampreneur must obtain (Table 3.2):

*   Semestre 1: min 14 points

    *   At least 14 skills at beginner level 1 or higher

*   Semestre 2: min 28 points

    *   At least 14 skills at beginner level 2 or higher

Table 3.1 Evaluation of the learning path module (1st year)

Parts of the module	Evaluation	Semester 1 (mid-September to end of January)		Semester 2 (mid-February to the end of June)	
		Minima	Maxima	Minima	Maxima
Dialogue Sessions (DS)	0.75 point per DS followed	21 points (28 DS)	24 points (32 DS)	21 points (28 DS)	24 points (32 DS)
Training Sessions (TS)	2 points per TS followed	12 points (6 TS)	-	10 points (5 TS)	-
Individual Readings (IR)	2 points for any presented and validated reading	12 points (6 books)	-	10 points (5 books)	-
Applied Projects (AP)	0.2 point per hour validated by the CP	40 points (200 h)	60 points (300 h)	20 points (100 h)	30 points (150 h)
Reflective Articles (RA)	5 points per AR (3 to 6 pages) validated by the coach	15 points (3 RA)	-	15 points (3 RA)	-
Learning Journey (LJ)	24 points for active participation in LJ			24[*] points (120 h)	24 points (120 h)
Minimum total		**100 points**		**100 points**	

[*]If part of the LJ is already performed during semester 1, the points are balanced with the APs (1 LJ day = 8 AP hours)
Source: Perruchoud, Emery, Rey, Cavin (2020a).

Table 3.2 Evaluation of the portfolio of competences module (1st year)

Evaluation	Semester 1 (mid-September to end of January)			Semester 2 (mid-February to the end of June)		
	Minima	*Maxima*		*Minima*	*Maxima*	
360° evaluation of the 21 competences (self-assessment, 3 to 5 teampreneurs drawn at random, coaches and experts)	Have achieved the levels mentioned above out of 21 competences	14 points (beginner 1)	-		28 points (beginner 2)	-

Source: Perruchoud, Emery, Rey, Cavin (2020a).

4 Fostering Students' Motivation to Be and Stay in Action

Olga Bourachnikova and
Caroline Merdinger-Rumpler

Introduction

The programme *Bachelor Team Entrepreneur* (BTE) at Business School of Strasbourg University has its roots in the pedagogical approach of Team Academy (TA). At the BTE, commitment to student action is the cornerstone of the programme, as lack of action implies lack of opportunity to learn and therefore to train. Since the creation of the BTE in 2011, the pedagogical team has noticed that the dynamic of action was irregular. This observation motivates our questioning in order to better understand how to support students' motivation to enter and stay in action so that the learning by doing process can take place (Kolb, 1984).

The subject of human motivation is defined as the set of energies underlying the process by which a person devotes intensity, direction, and persistence to a task in order to achieve a goal (Robbins & Judge, 2018). Our research is built on the Self-Determination Theory (SDT) of Ryan and Deci (2017), linking motivation to the specificities of the social environment. SDT identifies different types of motivation, grouped into two main categories: controlled motivation and autonomous motivation, also called self-determined motivation. In the case of autonomous motivation, behaviour is associated by the individual with the feeling of free choice, whereas in the case of controlled motivation, behaviour is associated with pressures and demands that the individual perceives to be external. The numerous empirical studies dedicated to SDT show that the development of autonomous motivation will result in an increase in individual well-being and performance. SDT lays down the conditions for the development of autonomous motivation based on the satisfaction of three basic psychological needs: the need for autonomy, the need to feel competent, and the need to connect with others. The psychological need for

DOI: 10.4324/9781003163114-5

autonomy refers to the possibility for the individual to act by exercising his or her will and free choice, or to the desire to organize and decide on his or her behaviour in such a way that his or her actions are in accordance with the "true self". The need to feel competent is part of a feeling of efficiency and control over one's environment. The need to connect with others refers to the desire to feel connected to others, especially to those who are important to us. The more the environment tends to satisfy those fundamental needs, the more the individual gets autonomously motivated.

The issue addressed in our research concerns the pedagogical challenges of supporting students of the BTE in the development of their autonomy. As BTE offers a significant amount of freedom to learners this means questioning the balance between the constraints and freedom offered to them by the pedagogical framework.

Precisely, we intended to explore:

- The way in which, in concrete terms, students experience the space of freedom of the BTE
- The challenges they face, particularly in relation to their action
- What it means for them to be autonomous

The 'BTE': A 10 years little sister within the Team Academy family

Over the period of our study, the case of the BTE of Strasbourg proves to be very interesting because the way the TA approach has been implemented until 2018 has given students a lot of freedom and seems to have satisfied students' need for autonomy. We present herewith the main specificities of the BTE in relation to our problematic:

- The evaluation is annual and aims at validating the competencies of the TA reference system, based on the elements in the student's portfolio. The evaluation of each competence is carried out through a dialogue between the student, two of his or her teammates, and the team coach. Mid-year assessments take place in January but do not have an impact on the final grade.
- The explicit requirements on the content of the portfolio are quantitative, with the student having a free choice of sources and themes (no imposed reading list, not pre-defined reflection paper topics). Each student must produce a certain number of learning contracts, essays, reflection papers, motorola visits, pre-defined by

the pedagogical framework. The validation process for portfolio papers is not explicitly and unambiguously determined.

*   Students are free to choose which projects they engage in and who with (e.g. working alone). The only restriction is the legal framework. The project does not need to be validated by the student's team. Project reports or monitoring of hours of action are not required.
*   The obligation to be present on the premises is limited to participation in Training Sessions by the student's team twice a week.

Methodology of the study

The study is based on 10 semi-structured interviews, lasting an average of one hour, conducted with 3 one-year graduates, 4 third-year students, and 3 second-year students.

The interview guide asked the students what it means to them to be *in action*, the main motivating factors that impact action (or inaction), and the elements of the BTE instructional design that have helped or hindered their action. The interviews were transcribed in full and processed according to the principles of thematic content analysis. All coding steps were carried out manually in double coding by two researchers working independently.

The findings will be structured as follows. When asked what autonomy at the BTE means to them, students will look at three different aspects. Firstly, students express how the BTE is a space of freedom for them. Secondly, they report on the consequences of this freedom for them, especially with regard to their actions. Finally, they make recommendations regarding the pedagogical framework.

The BTE: A space of freedom for students

Students came to the BTE, attracted by the freedom of the setting and the promise of an education without traditional courses *"autonomy is clearly at the heart of the BTE, I came partly for that"(50.36)*. This freedom is a freedom to choose, to decide, and this at time schedule, projects, and learning level:

> *"Clearly we can plan any way we want" (50.36).*

> *"They let us do the projects that everyone wants in the first place. As long as it's legal" (21.115).*

"No matter what you want to learn, you have the opportunity to learn it" (20.56).

"I am given the choice how I want to learn" (20.56).

Finally, the BTE's concept of freedom is based on action and learning and allows students to choose not only what they wish to achieve or learn (the what) but also how they are going to do it (the how).

The freedom of the framework will have two effects on commitment to action, what some will call the *"double-edged sword"(36.89)* of autonomy.

What does it mean to be autonomous?

Being autonomous means taking responsibility for one's choices, whether in action or inaction.

"You can choose not to be in action.(…) Technically spending a year doing nothing. You don't go into second year, but you can. It's up to you. On the other hand, when you make the choice to do nothing, in fact, it influences your personal life (…) And above all, it influences the team" (51.72).

On the other hand, when the period of inaction is perceived as too long for the student, and the associated state of unease becomes too much to bear, there is a risk of dropping out.

"… what is interesting and at the same time cruel is that there is this side «we know that there will be losses. » (…) That is to say that those who cannot bear this autonomy will leave" (24.71).

As far as action is concerned, it is not enough to be committed to action, but it is a matter of being committed to action in such a way as to be responsible for it by taking responsibility for the consequences of one's choices and actions on oneself and on others.

"And in fact, there are no excuses anymore either, if I'm not in action it's my fault, full stop. It's not the team's fault" (32.74).

For some students, the responsibility they take on will go beyond the academic framework of the course to include responsibility for their lives in the broadest sense. The training can therefore be seen as a preparation for an independent life, with its share of existential anguish.

"But I've never been as anxious as I have been since I've started the Bachelor because I realised that my life could have a meaning and that for the moment I wasn't really doing anything with it yet. And that's what scares me" (67.136).

The power to choose: A driving force to engage in action

"In the end I do a bit of what I want. I manage as I want to. In fact I've never worked so hard. I work every weekend, in the evenings when I get home, all the time actually" (6.75).

Students take action either to connect with their aspirations, their dreams and do what makes sense to them or to escape from the state of unhappiness caused by inaction.

"For me, there is a need for stakes. To take action, there must be either an issue that attracts me or that I see what I don't want to be and I run away from it. I need to feed myself. Or I'm attracted by a dream and I do everything I can for it, but the real motivation is that I can't afford to do nothing" (63.51).

They consciously implement strategies to achieve their goals. These strategies can affect their daily lives and go beyond the purely academic framework.

"The first is daily rituals. (...) Typically for example working at least three hours a day on my project, or getting up before 8am, or (...) Personal things like not smoking (...), doing sports etc. (...) It avoids, for example, getting up at noon and taking a nap at 2pm and watching films all day long" (59.80).

"And here, for example, I'm making a social readjustment. It means that people whom I like a lot I'm going to see less. Whereas I like them, but from a factual point of view they are people who have stopped studying (...) I have to make a social (...) so that my entourage are people who are related to my ambition" (34.7).

The power to choose: A problem

Students face situations where they do not necessarily know what to do, how to do it, or where to start.

> *"Because at the beginning, autonomy can push you to do nothing, because you just simply don't know what to do either, and so that's quite complicated" (46.102).*

> *"Choose your own goals. Really, I know it's a bit complicated. I personally can't reach my goals (...) or I don't know how to estimate how long it will take me to do it" (10.114).*

Being lost, they are unable to engage in action and fall into a period of varying degrees of inaction. Moments of inaction are generally badly experienced by students who characterize them as moments of anxiety, lack of joy, rumination, or waste of time.

> *"Inaction upon inaction, I was in a vicious circle in this project, I was simply starting to panic when I was doing nothing at all" (E2M 241).*

When the period of inaction comes to an end, the students experience the influence of a *trigger* which can be the student's awareness of the situation and the activation of his or her will, or the perception of an external threat strong enough to push for action.

> *"So, to go from 'no action' to 'action'... In fact, there was a trigger, but it came from me. It came out of nowhere else" (8.70).*

> *"In fact, repeating a year would have been a huge failure that I would have experienced badly and I think it would have been even more catastrophic if I had repeated a year. So, yes, I had no choice in fact. (...) Actually, I was really telling myself it's not on. You have to make it work" (25.137).*

Students' suggestions

The students are going to propose 3 main avenues relating to the framework that they feel is relevant to encourage the development of their autonomy: the progression of the framework over the 3 years of the course, the compulsory nature of a framework that encourages action, and the need to think about sanctions in the event of non-compliance with the framework.

Progression of the framework

Graduates or students at the end of their third year of study criticize the pedagogy by saying that it offers too much freedom at the beginning of the course. This freedom is sometimes perceived as *violent* by young people who have left mainstream education. They suggest a framework that offers a space of progressive freedom from one year to the next.

> *"In the beginning it was far too much for what I wanted. Clearly. (…) Since you are actually not yet able to handle such autonomy in your life (…) In this sense, it's super violent for some people. People who live in a family setting don't even know the price of pasta" (11.3).*

> *"In my case, what would have helped me a lot more is to have part of my autonomy taken away in the first year. (…) You can go back to the "classic system" and gradually remove this kind of thing where in the third year you have complete autonomy. I think that we could be 25% autonomous in the first year, 50% in the second year and 100% in the third year" (26.17).*

Encouraging but also constraining action

The main message from students is the importance of a framework that guides their action (what to do and how to do it) and constrains action to the point of forcing them out of their comfort zone.

> *"It's true that sometimes we lack the autonomy to do things we don't want to do, for example, sometimes in a project we have to go and see people, but if they don't tell us to do it, we'll try to push it as far as possible if it's something we don't necessarily like to do" (21.115).*

Sanctioning non-compliance

Students express the need for sanctions for non-compliance with the framework.

"When you have a company in which your boss tells you what to do or you're fired. This is when you understand what it is like to have constraints and to be responsible. However, in the Bachelor you have a lot of freedom but almost no sanctions. You can always get away with whatever you do" (2.64).

And so, what are the impacts on the pedagogical design?

Learning-by-doing or action learning pedagogies assume that the student is in action to learn. Thus, being in action is the central pillar of training. However, observation of student activity over ten years of the programme leads us to observe the systematic existence of periods of more or less long periods of inaction. This observation leads us, in our pedagogical practice, to question the conditions that ensure that periods of action, but also of inaction, are at the service of the development of students' autonomous motivation.

We present herewith our reflection and feedback on the identification of three pedagogical challenges for action learning-based training of the TA type. The first challenge directly addresses the student's involvement in the action. The second issue questions the challenge posed by the existence of periods of inaction. Finally, the third issue raises the question of supporting student autonomy by addressing the right balance to be found between laissez-faire and control/constraint in the chosen pedagogical system.

Supporting action and creating the conditions for learning

How to ensure regularity of action on the part of the student? How to promote a pedagogical design that encourages action and makes it visible? We suggest that the primary mission of the pedagogical framework is to push the student to DO and to SHOW what he/she has DONE so that he/she can develop his/her learning.

In the case of the BTE, the pedagogical team seems to have taken up the challenge of developing students' reflective skills. This is confirmed by the quality of the portfolio writings as well as the richness and depth of the reflective feedback provided by students in the interviews we conducted with them for this study. The hypothesis that we formulate to explain students' reflexivity is to have explained the requirements of the framework for students' reflexive productions (number of obligatory writings, validation of writings by coaches and peers...). On the other hand, the setting leaves students a great deal of freedom for all that concerns the action. This means that action is in reality not or only very little supervised. Thus, over the period of this study, indicators to measure commitment to action are non-existent at the BTE. It should be noted here that for BTE students, *being in action* is not systematically linked to entrepreneurial action in the context of a project, and is sometimes not even linked to training, but refers to the structuring of the student's time in his/her daily life, or even his/her personal life path (Bourachnikova & Merdinger-Rumpler, 2019).

As a result of the processing of these interviews and the results, we have modified the pedagogical framework. We have moved from an annual evaluation to a six-month evaluation mode. The underlying idea is to push the student into action by validating 2 semesters, based on the hypothesis that it would be more difficult for him/her to be inactive. At the same time, we have set up a pedagogical framework for the action with the integration of tools for monitoring the action, such as a project follow-up or a weekly hourly investment sheet. We also told the students that we expect them to respect a Fifty-action/ Fifty-learning time-sharing system. Thus, the student must show that around twenty hours per week are devoted to action.

Accepting inaction as a learning experience

If the student is in action, the reflective tools enable him/her to develop skills, make his/her own choices, and ultimately contribute to the development of his/her autonomy. What happens when the student is not in action? This period is described by students as uncomfortable, even provoking anxiety, and unbearable over a longer period of time. Students feel *lost*. Some of them then experience a trigger that allows them to get out of inaction. Although we have not explored the origin of this trigger, we can notice that when the inaction phase has been particularly difficult to live through, it sometimes serves as a *never again* experience for the student who has overcome it. The students' comments also lead us to realise that it seems that the period of inaction is related to the pedagogy of learning by doing and constitutes a key stage in the development of student autonomy.

The challenge is then to allow this stage to exist in the educational system so that the student can experience the *emptiness*, the *feeling of being lost*, from which he will be able to build himself, experience a trigger, and decide to commit himself. We can then speak of a *creative void*. Autonomy is then achieved through the existence of action–inaction loops that are experienced and overcome by the student throughout the training process. It is therefore not a question of preventing or denying these periods of inaction at all costs, but of making them part of the process of learning. The pedagogical framework must then support the student in becoming aware of his or her state with regard to ACTION by systematically asking the question of: Where do I stand? (am I or am I not in action?) What is happening inside me-for me? What are my needs?

In the case of the BTE, after observation of regular periods of inaction that was potentially destructive for the students, the first reaction of the teaching team was to impose a framework prohibiting inaction, opting for a shift to close control. We very quickly became aware of the discomfort that this engendered in some students, who neither experienced the trigger of salvation from inaction, nor the development of autonomy. We have therefore suggested fully accept the period of inaction and make it an integral part of the learning process in the BTE. In order to do this, we developed a tool that we called *the Phoenix project*. When the student becomes aware of his or her state of inaction, he or she is asked to engage in a Phoenix project which aims to accompany him or her during this period of inaction in order to maximize the probability that it will turn into a *fertile or creative void* and lead to the *trigger*. The student is then coached individually in a weekly appointment, with missions that are suggested so that he or she can accomplish a minimum of *active* hours per week. As this initiative has started recently, we do not yet have the necessary hindsight to analyze its effects, but it seems to move towards the right direction.

Finding the right balance between laissez-faire and constraints

The third pedagogical challenge questions the notion of the right balance between constraining-controlling and laisser-faire. What to impose and when to emancipate? How much freedom to do what exactly? At what points in the training programme?

If the student develops an awareness of his or her responsibility (in relation to himself or herself, to others – in particular, his or her team) and fully accepts the consequences of his or her action and inaction, this leads to the development of autonomy. In the case of a TA-type model, autonomy develops in the action–inaction loop allowed by the degree of freedom of the framework, combined with a reflection period allowing the student to develop his or her knowledge and skills. Let us observe two extreme cases.

The first situation is that of a student whose motivation is autonomous in the sense of Ryan & Deci (2017), which induces him/her to take responsibility for his/her action/inaction and the consequences in relation to his/her pedagogical environment. The freedom offered by the framework is a space that he or she will learn to manage and be devoted to in order to gain experiences and learn from them in a way that is constructive for him or her and his or her future.

In the second situation, the student has not developed sufficient autonomous motivation to put himself or herself into action. In this case, he or she does not do it because he or she does not feel sufficiently competent, whether this feeling is based on an objective assessment of his or her actual competence or not, because he or she is afraid to engage in the action because of a lack of self-confidence or because he or she does not feel like it, whether it is because he or she has not yet developed sufficient self-awareness to know what he or she likes to do or for some other reason. Here, the educational framework must accompany and support the student, pushing him or her to take action and develop skills and self-confidence. The pedagogical design must then be based on more control, with constraints and requirements accompanied by sanctions in order to hook the student's extrinsic motivation. Many aspects are at stake in this situation, including questions such as: Are the sanctions consistent with the intention of this type of emancipatory pedagogy? Are they perceived as trustworthy by the student? Are they supported by the entire teaching team in order to ensure the cohesion of the framework? How can the adaptation of the framework be cohesively accommodated to the individual and the group alike?

During the BTE training, students experience both described extreme situations. Even if the trend observed throughout the course is towards the development of autonomous motivation, the motivational process is far from being linear and identical for each student. In this way, it is possible for the student to review motivational phases based on more or less autonomous logic. Furthermore, the student may experience differentiated motivations according to the stages or activities linked to his or her action in the same project or in different projects by being motivated by internal dynamics for some (autonomous motivation) and by external pressures for others (controlled motivation). It seems to us, therefore, that one of the main keys to the success of the pedagogical design of a TA-type training course rests on two pillars. On the one hand, the adaptation of the framework to the motivational state of the student in order to avoid that it is deployed in an overly controlling way with students who have already developed sufficient autonomous motivation. On the other hand, the existence of a permanent dialogue with the student (and his or her team) and the establishment of full transparency both on the rules constituting the pedagogical framework and on the way in which they are implemented and decisions are taken.

Following the interviews, we conducted, we have modified the pedagogical framework of the BTE by integrating graduation of the space of freedom for both action and reflective activities. Thus, in the first year, the framework is controlled through projects imposed by the coaches and to be carried out in teams as well as through the explicit formalization of the number of pieces of each category of expected productions in the student's portfolio. In the second year, the framework offers more freedom of action, in that the missions are no longer imposed but proposed while maintaining requirements for reflexive work. In the third year, autonomy is very high: Projects are free of choice and portfolio objectives are allocated to each student within his or her team.

In conclusion, our study shows that in order to sustain the students' learning in an action-learning cycle, the pedagogical framework has to guide action, accept and support inaction as a relevant learning experience, and finally to find a dynamic balance between laissez-faire and constraints.

References

Bourachnikova, O. & Merdinger-Rumpler, C. (2019). Quels enjeux pédagogiques pour une formation entrepreneuriale fondée sur l'apprentissage par l'action? *Entreprendre & Innover*, *3*(42–43), pp. 61–71. 10.3 917/entin.042.0061.

Kolb, D. (1984). *Experiential Learning: Experience as a source of learning and development*. NJ: Prentice Hall.

Robbins, S.P. & Judge, T.A. (2018). *Organizational Behavior*. 18th edition. Pearson.

Ryan, R. M. & Deci, E. L. (2017). *Self-determination theory. Basic psychological needs in motivation, development and wellness*. NY: Guilford Press.

5 Developing a Sister Programme — The First of its Kind

Polly Wardle

Introduction

This research aims to enhance the reader's knowledge and understanding of developing partner programmes at Higher Education (HE) level, using a Team Academy methodology. This research reports the experiences and opinions of staff from Bristol City Robins Foundation (BCRF) and The University of the West of England (UWE), who were involved in the development and implementation of the BA (Hons) Sports Business and Entrepreneurship (SBE) programme.

BCRF, the official charity of Bristol City Football Club, was in 2016 approached to develop the SBE programme in association with UWE. At this time, UWE had been successfully running a BA (Hons) Business Team Entrepreneurship (TE) programme since 2013, a ground-breaking programme within UWE's business school, using a Team Academy methodology. The SBE programme is the first known worldwide example of an HE institution developing a sister programme, using Team Academy methodology within a different setting, in this case, sport.

By Team Academy standards, the TE programme offered at UWE, Frenchay campus is a large programme, with 60 students, known as Team Entrepreneurs (TEs) at each level (year). This makes up a total programme cohort of up to 180 TEs. In comparison, the SBE programme at Ashton Gate Stadium has 20 TEs at each level, with a maximum of 60 TEs on the programme. Both SBE and TE programmes are inspired by Team Academy a model developed in 1993, founded in Finland by Johannes Partanen at Jyvaskyla University of Applied Sciences. Team Academy is unlike "traditional" education, it challenges students to a new way of learning and has been proved influential within Finland and internationally (Tosey et al., 2015). The model's focus is mainly on team learning, aligning and developing the

DOI: 10.4324/9781003163114-6

capacity of a team to create the results its members genuinely wish for, through developing skills of dialogue (Isaacs, 1999) and learning through doing. A strong relationship between action and reflection is built. TEs create action through projects, whilst critically reflecting on learning in training sessions. Their team company is the vehicle for learning and the Team Academy model requires TEs to create and operate a variety of real enterprises which they will own and control (Leinonen et al., 2004; Heikkinen 2003).

Research methodology

I have conducted this research as Programme Leader of the SBE programme. Within this piece of research, I have used an illuminative evaluation methodology (Parlett & Hamilton, 1972). Illuminative evaluation methodology was developed for use in educational settings based on sociology and looks at innovation in education (Parlett & Hamilton, 1972). Unlike other evaluation methodologies, an illuminative approach provides a range of information and flexibility. Instead of a focus on testing (Gordon 1991), illuminative evaluation has a focus on details such philosophy of the programme, programme objectives, goals, and course content. This type of evaluation has a dual focus: the instructional system, such as assumptions, and the learning milieu, such as experiences and contributions of stakeholders.

The main aim of this research was to achieve an in-depth understanding of staff experiences developing and implementing the SBE programme. As an insider researcher, I was in a unique position to draw upon shared understandings of the participants, and research this area whilst holding much prior knowledge about it (Mercer, 2007). This meant that it was easier to gain acceptance and trust, with shorter preparation time as I was already in the 'field' of study (Costley et al., 2010). However, this can bring an experience of role conflict and a bias towards the interpretation and findings of the research (Saidin, 2016), thus acknowledging I will not be able to hold an exclusively unbiased approach when collecting and interpreting my data.

No singular method of data analysis is associated with an illuminative evaluation methodology (Taylor & Medina, 2013), I, therefore, elected to utilize focus groups as this provided me with the opportunity to involve a greater number of participants in a shorter length of time (Berg 2001). The participants could share narratives, express opinions, and have discussions, allowing challenge of each other and a building onto each other's experiences and views. Due to a small number of people being meaningfully involved in the planning and implementation of the

SBE programme, the sample available was very small. I aimed to involve individuals from both organizations who hold a wide range of experiences from the programme set up, not just those from one organization. I identified 4 individuals who were heavily involved in the programme, 2 from BCRF, and 2 from UWE to gain both perspectives of the programme's implementation and decided to hold a focus group with these people. I will refer to them as (I1, BCRF), (I2, BCRF), (I3, UWE), and (I4, UWE).

My evaluation was summative and the evaluation questions were:

1   How can the implementation of a Team Academy methodology be improved?
2   What is the nature of the relationship between UWE and BCRF and its resulting impact on the SBE programme?
3   What are the ethical considerations when working in partnership and how do you effectively manage for these?

As an organization, BCRF is a charity which aims to improve lives through football and learning. It was noted that the SBE programme fits into the vision of the organization and Education department, aiming to create opportunities and empower participants.

"We didn't want to write a new course. We wanted to develop a different type of HE provision that we currently do not cater for. It was a perfect fit to take a brilliant TE course and adapt it to suit us" (I1, BCRF).

In the following section, we will talk about the programme implementation, including assessing barriers and enablers to implementation and identifying strategies for change of practice.

Enablers to implementation

First and foremost, it was highlighted to partner with an institution that aligns with your values and shares the purpose as to why the course is being developed.

"I would recommend to partner with an institute that shares your purpose and values. This aids the relationship that you are trying to foster" (I2, BCRF).

Through the data collected it was recognized that the two institutes met early to talk about the programme, and felt they built the programme together.

> *"In my opinion, this is the best example of partnership work that we have got at UWE. It was a genuine partnership where we worked together to design and map the programme, allowing BCRF to make it fit with their vison and context"* (I3, UWE).

Rezania and Lingham (2009) claim that factors, such as planning and designing with individuals, building rapport, establishing trust, and building credibility, contribute to a successful long-term relationship. It was also recognized that UWE worked with BCRF to help them develop their capacities to deliver the programme, allowing discounted access to Masters modules for staff development and access to learn from the current TE course.

> *"You immersed yourselves in UWE as an institution and the TE course on a weekly basis. You had space to think about how these experiences related to what you wanted to set up and you liked or wanted to change for your own context"* (I4, UWE).

The staff programme team of SBE was also identified as enablers. This immersion and open-mindedness of SBE staff allowed knowledge and understanding of the programme and methodology to grow, as well as an openness to opportunities to enable the course to develop. It was also identified that the new programme was built using the methodology of the UWE programme. This is highlighted as an important insight and something to share with others who might find themselves developing a programme of this kind. It is not only the TEs that experience the methodology of the programme, programme staff are also living by the methodology and have to trust the process too.

A clear enabler that was identified was the geographical location of the two partners being 7 miles apart. It was discussed that the close locations had enabled partnership working that would have been harder remotely, allowing trusting relationships to be built in person (Houman-Andersen & Kumar 2006). Built onto this was the ability to have link tutors working with the SBE programme staff team. A link tutor from UWE would join the SBE weekly staff meeting. This allowed support and advice to be given when needed. This link tutor was someone who had been through the process of setting up the UWE TE course so could reassure, share insights, and help develop and progress the SBE programme and staff, whilst allowing a programme identity to grow. Having an open and honest relationship with a link tutor who was accessible was a key enabler and an important aspect of the implementation which is discussed later.

Barriers to implementation and suggestions of future change

Through the data collected it was clear that the participants felt there were barriers to the implementation of the programme. Firstly, it was noted that BCRF had inexperience in running education programmes at the university degree level.

"Our organisation processes and procedures are different to UWE, we're not an educational institute alone. It took time to read and research to ensure we were in the right position when we started" (I1, BCRF).

BCRF staff noted during the first year of the programme they were always learning. There was always something new to do until they got to induction of second year and knew they had been through the processes of everything once. Everyone has always got to have a first time they do something, but it was suggested to try not to make this type of programme the first HE programme, due to the complex nature of the methodology.

Finally, it was also identified that the proximity and closeness of UWE and TE courses also brought its barriers.

"There was huge safety from the partner programme as it was so close. This was relied on and sometimes it might not have been the right thing to do. If that programme was not there, would you have had the confidence to do things differently?" (I4, UWE).

This is an important insight, and although it has brought good learning and enabled the SBE programme to be where it is now, it would be recommended to other programmes starting out to be aware of this from the outset. This reflection resonated with all participants who were heavily involved in the first year of the programme and the suggestion for other organizations who will be creating similar partnerships is to try and create their own identity. It took SBE as a programme team a year to recognize that they could be as similar or as different to the UWE TE programme as they wanted. The SBE programme staff felt they were too worried that the programme was straying too far from the methodology in the first year. Whereas on reflection, they were worried they were straying too far from UWE's TE programme identity.

The current situation in relation to the programme's *proposed* implementation

It was discussed that one of the main reasons the SBE programme was set up by BCRF was to give opportunity to young adults in Bristol. BCRF wanted to offer this as a pathway from their current post 16 education courses as well as giving opportunity to wider Bristol-based students, offering a type of provision that might benefit students who first thought traditional HE was not appropriate to them. Nearly 4 years later, this is still seen as the reason for the programme's existence and is the driving force when making decisions about the programme. Although it was noted that applicants to the programme are coming from all over the UK and world, India and South Africa for example, with only 10–20% of applicants on a yearly basis coming from the Bristol area. This shows there is still marketing work to do within Bristol to expose this programme to the intended audience. The programme team are aware of this and working with a newly appointed marketing and communications executive within the organization as to how to approach this.

It was noted that UWE wanted to grow the programme to double or triple the number of TEs joining each year. UWE is hoping for the programme to grow to 40–50 TEs joining each year, compared to BCRF wanting around 30 TEs joining each year. BCRF sees the benefits that having smaller cohorts allowing increased opportunity for TEs within the Bristol Sport group, working on real challenges and issues for the organization. Scaling up the programme could also result in quality concerns with increased numbers of learners (Buhl et al., 2018). Scaling up is something that BCRF would like to do, but only when the quality of the programme can be ensured. Applications onto the programme have increased from 30 in the first year, to nearly 130 in its 4th year. It was discussed this was due to increased marketing and visibility on UWE webpages. However, the number of applicants accepting their place on the programme is staying similar each year, around the 20 mark. Participants felt the generic name of the degree programme appeals to a wide audience of applications, but unfortunately this does not yet translate into higher conversation rates into the programme.

It was also discussed that SBE programme team was disillusioned when seeing the UWE TE programme TEs and businesses produced.

"I personally thought that things would happen quickly and actually it's a slower process. I am now much more realistic about expectations and success of the TEs, unlike previously thinking we'd be seeing businesses within 3 months" (I1, BCRF).

This was identified as a big learning point for everyone on the SBE staff team, with larger more complex businesses only starting to show now 3 years into the programme. The programme team also reflected that the "big showcase businesses" are not the only outcome now hoped for the TEs on the programme. Instead, there is a shift in mindset from staff encouraging other enterprising and entrepreneurial activities that don't always result in the outcome of setting up a business but still result in heavy learning and personal development.

All participants also said that the programme has stayed true to the methodology.

"I think your programme is the closest in the UK to the Finnish model. The people and the philosophy of BCRF is in tune with Finland" (I4, UWE).

This was highlighted as positive, and it was also discussed that the methodology is having a bigger impact on the wider organization than was previously expected at implementation stage. The methodology of the programme is being used in different departments of BCRF organization. An example of that is using the tool of check-in and check-out of team meetings, and wider dialogue on issues rather than top-down approaches. Importantly, the willingness to give and receive feedback from other members within the organization has enabled an effective learning process whilst using the methodology (Popper & Lipshitz, 2000), adapting as they go.

The relationship between UWE and BCRF and its impact on the SBE programme

Rosser (2018) argues that it is not organizations or institutions that create successful partnerships but the relationships of people within these and how we approach and engage with each other. Mutual respect is key to success along with an open and receptive attitude and a belief that everyone can learn from others (Spies et al., 2015). The relationships developed between the staff of BCRF and UWE were highlighted as incredibly strong and important to the development and progression of the programme. It was discussed that "on the ground" relationships between module leaders and programme staff are strong, and so too past this level with executive members of staff of both partner organizations. Engaging in the process of creating and sustaining relationships involves substantial emotional investment and effort (Hargreaves, 2000). It was identified by participants that a genuine two-way collaborative relationship has been formed between the two institutions, with emotional investment and effort from both sides.

In discussions, it was highlighted that the SBE programme team handled situations effectively with UWE. The SBE programme recognizes its own identity and does not feel they have to mirror the TE programme when they feel as though it is not the right thing to do. This has meant that the programme has benefitted from decisions and developed the programme in the way which suited their progression and environment, whilst managing the relationship between both programmes effectively.

"As link tutor I feel I hold a large role as bridge between both programmes, knowing both parties well I can help translate so both programmes relationships are fostered and understand what is being said" (I4, UWE).

Through discussions, it was clear that the link tutor role is seen as paramount importance and the relationships that they made with the programme staff enabled this. Farmer (2015) argues that the approach and way of a person towards others has a huge impact. This link tutor has developed an authentic, trustworthy relationship enabling BCFR staff to feel they are in a safe, holding environment. This enables BCRF staff to try ideas and make mistakes without the fear of failure or prejudice, feel safe to contribute, be honest, and disclose sensitive feelings and information in complete confidentiality. This authentic relationship improved staff performance, satisfaction, and well-being (Clapp-Smith, Vogelgesang & Avey, 2009). Shamir and Eilam (2005) argue that authentic leadership is something that results from life experience and cannot be trained. This link tutor has gone through the process of setting up a programme of this methodology, building UWE TE programme, so has life experience in this area to support and guide BCRF staff in its early stages and beyond.

The positive relationship held between both programmes and organizations has had an impact on the SBE programme. Through discussions, it was clear that BCRF feels that they are trusted to develop the programme in a way that utilizes their environment and unique selling points. This has meant that the SBE programme looks and operates in a different manner from the TE programme in some ways. The SBE programme can offer project activities utilizing the environment of Bristol Sport and the professional organizations that run out of the stadium. The TEs have worked on real-life challenges within departments and networked with experts.

Ethical issues in partnership working and how these can be managed

There are many ethical issues surrounding partnership work (Braaten, 2018). This includes issues such as contracting (Gettman, Edinger & Wouters, 2019), integrity (Passmore, Peterson & Freire, 2013), confidentiality (Turner & Hawkins, 2016), and conflict of interest (Burger & Van Coller-Peter, 2019).

> *"As link tutor I have to be careful, working closely with both SBE and TE. I need to maintain clean hands, have trust and confidentiality, staying independent yet I am really involved. I have competing interests at times"* (I4, UWE).

Smith and Fitzpatrick (1995) argue that relationships can carry potential challenges, issues with boundaries, roles, conflict of interest, and confidentiality. Agreeing a contract is important as it will outline appropriate boundaries with individuals and specific goals (De Haan et al., 2011). This is something that UWE's link tutor did with the SBE programme team when conducting supervision sessions and attending team meetings.

> *"The proximity of the courses could have been an ethical issue. We do not want to feel we are taking prospective students from the UWE TE programme"* (I2, BCRF).

This conflict was recognized by everyone and could have arisen, but this has been managed well. At open days and student-facing events, programme leaders of both courses sell the methodology and the programme together, explaining the contextual difference between the two programmes and allowing prospective students to make their own minds up around which course and features might suit the applicant the most. Each year both programmes now have more than 100 student applicants. Yearly, only around 10 students apply to both programmes, with last year only 2 of those 10 accepting an offer on either programme. This shows minimal conflict of interest, and evidence that the SBE programme is reaching and attracting an audience that UWE TE programme is not currently touching.

"It's been important for us to recognise the risk that we pose to UWE and the responsibilities we have to them. Not only as a sister programme to TE, but also a brand and network. The partnership boards have been useful talking about ethical issues and having the risk register. I feel we have processes in place to think about these things and talk about them as a group" (I1, BCRF).

Finally, it was noted that the development of the programme, including potential risks and ethical issues, are highlighted and discussed at a partnership board which takes place every 6 months. A partnership board is a space where both BCRF and UWE staff join to communicate developments of the programme, share best practices, and raise any ethical or delivery issues which can be discussed openly utilizing both institutions' resources to resolve.

Conclusions

Many key learnings have emerged from this research. Hopefully, the reflections in this section will help other institutions that are applying TA methods and might be setting up similar partnership programmes.

It is important to select a partner that aligns with your values and purpose of what you want to achieve with the new programme. Once you have identified your institution to partner with, aim to build the relationship within the partnership as early as you can. Doing this on as many levels as possible, from module and programme leaders, finance to executive staff allows relationships to develop with relevant personnel.

Another learning highlighted was to try to work with an institution within reasonable proximity to you, allowing you to immerse yourself in their current programme as well as have accessible support on hand to develop your capacities to deliver the programme.

It was discussed that a partnership that was based 50 miles away would struggle to develop these relationships and would be harder to immerse themselves in the institution's current programme or receive quality support from a link tutor. Ensuring a clear link tutor role from someone within the partner institution was key learning taken, but more importantly, the more time, resources, experience, and passion the link tutor has to give to the programme the better position you will be in. The link tutors available for the SBE programme, their experience, and relationships built were seen as the single biggest enabler after the programme's implementation and continued development from the participants in the research.

It was also highlighted to ensure staff on the programme are open-minded, comfortable with ambiguity, and open to letting the methodology of the programme guide the journey. Participants discussed that you rarely feel in control in the early stages of the programme's implementation and trusting that process is hard to do but imperative for the programme's organic growth. Gaining feedback from partners, TEs, and each other is an integral part of any development, increasing performance, confidence, and self-awareness (Gregory et al., 2008). For the programme to be effective and maintainable, it must be reviewed often, as part of the reflective process of the learning relationship (Farmer, 2015). A key learning was the importance of the programme's quarterly strategy days, reviewing progress against goals. Participants stressed the importance of allowing your programme to grow in its own unique way in your setting. You could be different or similar to your partner's environment but allow your own programme identity to show and do not feel like you have to stick to the processes and methods of your partner programme. The mixture of your staff, TEs, environment, and USPs will create a programme that carries different experiences to your partner programme. Take what you think works well for you and change what you feel does not suit you. The important thing to stay true to is the identity of the methodology, not the identity of others from who you have learned from.

Finally, partners should be open to letting the methodology of the programme affect wider parts of the organization if there was opportunity, seeing the benefit of the methodology to not only the programme in question but also the wider organization. The research shows that it was not an easy and straightforward process of implementing and developing a programme of this nature and methodology, however, it was highlighted that the process has been very rewarding.

References

Berg, B.L. (2001). *Qualitative research methods: For the social sciences.* 4th ed. Boston: Pearson.

Braaten, E. (2018) *Ethical issues in education.* London: Sage.

Buhl, M., Andreasen, L.B., & Pushpanadham, K. (2018). Upscaling the number of learners, fragmenting the role of teachers: How do massive open online courses (MOOCs) form new conditions for learning design? *International Review of Education, 64*, pp. 179–195.

Burger, Z., & Van Coller-Peter, S. (2019). A guiding framework for multi-stakeholder contracting in executive coaching. *Journal of Human Resource Management, 17*(10), pp. 1–11. 10.4102/sajhrm.v17i0.1114.

Clapp-Smith, R., Vogelgesang, G.R., & Avey, J.B. (2009). Authentic leadership and positive psychological capital: The mediating role of trust at the group level of analysis. *Journal of Leadership and Organisational Studies, 15*(3), pp. 227–240.

Costley, C., Elliot, G., & Gibbs, P. (2010). *Doing Work Based Research.* London: Sage.

De Haan, E., Culpin, V., & Curd, J. (2011). "Executive coaching in practice: What determines helpfulness for clients of coaching?" *Personnel Review, 40*(1), pp. 24–44. 10.1108/00483481111095500.

Farmer, S. (2015). Making sense of team coaching. *The Coaching Psychologist, 11*(2), pp. 72–80.

Gettman, H.J., Edinger, S.K., & Wouters, K. (2019). Assessing contracting and the coaching relationship: Necessary infrastructure? *International Journal of Evidence-Based Coaching and Mentoring, 17*(1), pp. 46–62.

Gordon, K.H. (1991). Improving practice through illuminative evaluation. *Social Service Review, 65*(3), pp. 557–579. 10.1086/603853.

Gregory, J.B., Levy, P.E., & Jeffers, M. (2008). Development of a model of the feedback process within executive coaching. *Consulting Psychology Journal: Practice and Research, 60*(1), pp. 42–56. 10.1037/1065-9293.60.1.42.

Hargreaves, A. (2000). Mixed emotions: teachers' perceptions of their interactions with students. *Teaching and Teacher Education, 16*, pp. 811–826. 10.1016/s0742-051x(00)00028-7.

Heikkinen, H. (2003). Team Academy: A story of a school that learns. *Development and Learning in Organizations: An International Journal, 17*(1), pp. 7–9. 10.1108/13697230310458495.

Houman-Andersen, P., & Kumar, R. (2006). Emotions, trust and relationship development in business relationships: A conceptual model for buyer–seller dyads. *Industrial Marketing Management, 35*(4), pp. 522–535. 10.1016/j.indmarman.2004.10.010.

Isaacs, W.N. (1999). *Dialogue and the art of thinking together.* New York: Doubleday.

Leinonen, N., Partanen, J., & Palviainen, P. (2004) *The Team Academy: A true story of a community that learns by doing.* Jyväskylä: PS-kustannus.

Mercer, J. (2007). The challenges of insider research in educational institutions: Wielding a double-edged sword and resolving delicate dilemmas. *Oxford Review of Education, 33*(1), pp. 1–17. 10.1080/03054980601094651.

Parlett, M. Hamilton, D. (1972) *Evaluation as illumination: A new approach to the study of innovatory programmes.* Occasional paper 9. Scotland: Centre for Research in the Educational Science, University of Edinburgh.

Passmore, J., Peterson, D. B., & Freire, T. (2013). *The Wiley-Blackwell handbook of the psychology of coaching and mentoring.* London: Wiley-Blackwell.

Popper, M., & Lipshitz, R. (2000). Organisational learning: Mechanisms, culture, and feasibility. *Management Learning, 31*(2), pp. 181–196. 10.4135/9781446211571.n3.

Rezania, D., & Lingham, T. (2009). Coaching IT project teams: a design toolkit. *International Journal of Managing Projects in Business, 2*(4), pp. 577–590. 10.1108/17538370910991151.

Rosser, E. (2018). The importance of relationships in international collaborations. *British Journal of Nursing, 27*(13), pp. 761. 10.12968/bjon.2018.2 7.13.761.

Saidin, K. (2016). Insider researcher: Challenges and opportunities. *International Seminar on Generating Knowledge Through Research*, pp. 849–854. 10.21070/picecrs.v1i1.563

Shamir, B., & Eilam, G. (2005). "What's your story?" A life-stories approach to authentic leadership development. *The Leadership Quarterly, 16*(3), pp. 395–417. 10.1108/s1479-357120180000009017.

Smith, D. & Fitzpatrick, M. (1995). Patient–therapist boundary issues: An integrative review of theory and research. *Professional Psychology: Research and Practice, 26*, pp. 499–506. 10.1037/0735-7028.26.5.499.

Spies, L.A., Gamer, S.L., & Prater, L. (2015). Building global nurse capacity through relationships, education and collaboration. *Nurse Education Today, 35*(5), pp. 653–656. 10.1016/j.nedt.2015.01.014.

Taylor, P.C., & Medina, M.N.D. (2013). Educational research paradigms: From positivism to multiparadigmatic. *Journal for Meaning-Centred Education, 1*, pp. 1–16.

Tosey, P., Dhaliwal, S., & Hassinen, J. (2015). The Finnish Team Academy model: Implications for management education. *Management Learning, 46*(2), pp. 175–194. 10.1177/1350507613498334.

Turner, E., & Hawkins, P. (2016). Multi-stakeholder contracting in executive/business coaching: An analysis of practice and recommendations for gaining maximum value. *International Journal of Evidence-Based Coaching and Mentoring, 14*(2), pp. 48–65. 10.4324/9780429452031-5.

6 Exploring a Hybrid Approach of Team Academy Model in the Conventional Entrepreneurship Postgraduate Programme

Nan Jiang

Introduction

The growth of entrepreneurship education (EE) over the last 30 years is so rapid that *"our understanding of what should be taught by entrepreneurship educators, how it should be taught, and how outcomes should be assessed"* is upon critical reflection (Neck & Corbett, 2018, p. 9). Holding the belief that *"entrepreneurship education has an impact, not just on an informed intent to be an entrepreneur but also as a life skill"* (Krueger, 2015, p. 6), some entrepreneurship educators pioneered at *"moving away from pedagogy and traditional pedagogical approaches"*; that is, *"focus less on students gaining content knowledge about entrepreneurship but instead focus more on developing the entrepreneurial mindset"* (p. 6). Many believed that *"the key to those deep impacts is experiential learning"* (Krueger & Welpe, 2014). According to OECD report (Krueger, 2015), the leading-edge entrepreneurship programmes, including these Team Academy programmes (Tosey et al., 2015), would claim no longer teaches students about entrepreneurship instead teaching them to do entrepreneurship. However, the delivery of truly experiential learning has faced many institutional constraints and practical obstacles. Many conventional programmes are highly resistant to even the idea of *flipped* classroom (Krueger, 2015), let alone these innovative approaches we take for granted in the Team Academy (TA) programmes to implement experiential learning. Scholars and educators are concerned about the lack of reflexive and critical approaches at the level of educational practice and research in the field of EE (Fayolle, 2018).

In this book chapter, I provide a small glimpse into the insights of implementing TA approaches into conventional programme structures. Our classrooms are often unique and do not have the familiar conventional structure, which has probably led to the sceptical view on the

DOI: 10.4324/9781003163114-7

innovative methodology of TA. To open up our classroom to external review, I *"take a more critical stance, breaking away from the far too common 'taken for granted' position"* (Fayolle, 2018, p. 692) to make sense of my experience. As a team coach, I implemented team-oriented experiential learning in the Entrepreneurial Leadership and Management module in a conventionally structured postgraduate EE programme in a UK university. The discussion of this chapter is to critically reflect on my challenging experience to fully adopt the TA approach. The reflection is centred on the plausibility of a hybrid strategy to design short-term and simulated projects that have rendered effective experiential learning that can naturally foster entrepreneurial mindset and skills. As a result, I share my observations and a few practical insights to overcome institutional constraints and co-immerse with the other conventional modules in the same course in order to embrace innovative TA approaches. In the end, I suggest areas for future endeavours and exploration.

A challenging opportunity to implement Team Academy Model in UK Universities

There is increasing demand for EE that aims to enhance entrepreneurial competences in the UK, since the Quality Assurance Agency for Higher Education suggested the *"… call for a greater emphasis on enterprise and entrepreneurship education is compelling. Driven by a need for flexibility and adaptability, the labour market requires graduates with enhanced skills who can think on their feet and be innovative in a global economic environment"* (QAA, 2018, p 2). In response to such demand, many UK universities sought to introduce a distinct mode of teaching and learning that differs from the convention that existed in their business, management, and enterprise courses (Blackwood et al., 2015). In contrast to the constantly growing demand for programmes providing experiential learning that is believed would lead to entrepreneurial behaviours, entrepreneurship educators are under the pressure to overcome the constraints that *traditional* EE pedagogy has and seek for alternatives (Donnellon et al, 2014). Both researchers (Donnellon et al., 2014) and practitioners (Krueger, 2009) have observed the general lack of effective programme design that provides the real context for EE.

In this diverse landscape of EE in the UK, educational institutions and industrial organizations across the world are interested in experimenting innovative approaches in EE, such as learn by doing and coaching student-led team projects, which we advocate in the TA approach towards experiential learning (Halttunen, 2006). Increasingly, we discovered that experiential programmes could be powerful and imperative to enhance skills and competences (Blackwood et al., 2015). In addition, Krueger (2015) studied 26 OECD showcase programmes and reported that highly experiential entrepreneurship programmes that are remarkably immersed in the local entrepreneurial ecosystem (including the institutional stakeholder) can facilitate deep entrepreneurial learning. The TA model that was originally developed at Finland's Jyväskylä University of Applied Science's (Leinonen et al., 2004) has also been introduced to the UK. The key methodology in TA model promotes *a flexible learning approach*, such as learn by doing and coaching student-led team projects, to alter the lecturer-led conventional structured classroom lecturing (Tosey et al., 2015).

Following these principles, I took an opportunity in my current institution to design a new degree of MSc Enterprise and Innovation in September 2018 and launch it in 2019, during which I was appointed to advise on course development and validation. When the course was validated, I was given the opportunity to develop the module of Entrepreneurial Leadership and Management. My initial attempt was to fully adopt TA model in this module to provide students the experience of experiential learning. The plan did not start without any criticism, which helped my reflection to change and adapt the TA module in the later stage and create a hybrid design. When going through the literature, I discovered many shared concerns and opinions on adopting the innovative methodology of TA model:

Lack of legitimacy

As stated in the OECD report of entrepreneurial education (2015, p. 7):

> *"Entrepreneurship programmes love to say they no longer teach students about entrepreneurship, we are now teaching them to do entrepreneurship: An admirable but not well-defined goal. Nor have we measured actual impact. To say that we are now building the "entrepreneurial mindset" is insufficient if we cannot (or do not) be rigorous about what that term means both theoretically and empirically".*

Many reviewers of my proposal (to adopt the full TA model) would share this view to a certain extent. Due to the lack of theoretical underpinning and programme design maturity, the TA model appears to be marginalized in UK university entrepreneurship programmes. It is considered to be too radically innovative to become the alternative to the conventional approach, or suitable for the diverse needs of students, neither to be recognized as a possible solution for the trends of changing expectations in the UK.

This is a real problem for educators who wish to meet such aspiration of TA, as to present challenges to a strong continuum of established institutions that practice EE in the conventional fashion is complicated. When designing an entrepreneurship postgraduate programme, we need to answer many questions, such as how experiential shall the curriculum be? More importantly, how do we embed the practice of entrepreneurial team and community of learning in the conventional programme to render effective learning that is, to naturally foster entrepreneurial mindset and skills?

Lack of critical stance

Another common issue and feedback we obtain when trying to adopt TA is the question around the methodological rigour and the lack of critical approach. Critical studies and approaches are generally missing in EE and we often *"do not question (our) approaches, assumptions and practices"* (Fayolle, 2018, p. 697) so we should not be reluctant to look out and borrow concepts or methods from other fields. This critical stance shall be applied to both conventional and innovative EE programmes. This is confirmed in the report of OECD Centre for Entrepreneurship, SME, Regions, and Cities (2015, p. 7) that examine the effectiveness of entrepreneurial education programmes that claim to adopt experiential learning approach in practice:

> *"We will know it [mindset] when we see it" or simply assume that it is the necessary outcome from experiential learning. Very few programmes make any effort to assess mindset beyond entrepreneurial action or intent toward entrepreneurial action. In any event, it is rare to see any congruence between the definition and metrics. It is truism in education that we get what we measure or, if you prefer, it is hard to get what we are not aiming for".*

We often assume the absolute correlation between entrepreneurial mindset and skills and experiential learning, but rarely do we have evidence to prove this; in fact, we have not developed a constructive model to measure and assess the impact on behaviours. We need not only to have courage to disrupt established views and practice to create opportunities for promoting TA models but also challenge our own assumptions. We shall be observant and honest on how effective the TA approach is to revolute the conventional constraints on the development of EE towards meeting new demands on our students.

A hybrid approach to entrepreneurship education in a UK Postgraduate Programme

In this section, I take a critical stance to present a postgraduate level Entrepreneurial Leadership and Management module in a UK University as a case study to discuss a strategy to embrace innovative TA approaches in the conventional teaching institution. The outputs, process, and inputs of the module are assessed to understand the level of interventions in this type of hybrid programme. In particular, the issues for exploration are:

- How do we motivate less independent learners to take ownership of their learning?
- How do we develop partnerships with the local and international entrepreneurial community for peer support?
- How do we collect learning evidence and communicate this to management while running the module?

According to the perspective of resolving conflicting institutional logics, the total removal of one logic that dominates the institutional culture (deinstitutionalization) in fact does not appear more attractive (Asangansi, 2012). A transitional strategy or dialectical strategy resolves conflicts *"through switching the project from one logic to the other without necessarily destroying the other logic, which perhaps, continues to exist elsewhere"* (Asangansi, 2012, p. 18). This seems to be more effective in my attempt to introduce TA approaches in a conventional EE programme. I share a few examples of how this hybrid design resolves institutional conflicts underlying between the full TA model and the conventional pedagogy and explain the impact on improving the legitimacy and critical stance to adopt the TA model in EE (in Table 6.1).

Transitional resolution strategy

The conflict resolution theory describes the transitional strategy as a resolution *"when actors need to focus on one logic and compromise the*

Table 6.1 Examples of institutional conflicts and resolution strategy from the case of EE

Institutional conflicts in conventional EE and ideal TA	Inference from case and literature	Resolutions	Resolution types
Pedagogy vs. Heutagogy	The role of the student is dependent or independent	Simulating instead of full experiential approach	Transitional resolution strategy
	Learning outcome is entrepreneurial intention or startup	Mindset and skills	Transitional resolution strategy
	Educator or students is in the centre of the learning	Shared and co-creation instead of student-led	Dialectical resolution strategy
	The role of the educator as a lecturer or a facilitator	Teaching plus peer coaching led by TA students	Dialectical resolution strategy

Source: Author's own.

other (not necessarily obliterate it)" (Asangansi, 2012, p. 18). Guided by this strategic perspective, I have identified a few key platforms within conventional institutional teaching and learning structure to showcase the TA approaches, in order to increase the awareness of management, colleagues, and students on alternative approaches for EE. First, the implementation of full TA model might be perceived being risky by the management, but we could carve space outside the conventional classroom to engage students with the TA experience that are complementary to the classroom learning. For example, I mentor students to found the Entrepreneurship Society. The society is a vehicle to encourage student-led team projects that provide opportunities for students to engage with the real practice of entrepreneurship. Through being coached to organize and manage society-related activities, the students have established interdependent relationships that positively impact their classroom interactions and their attitude towards teamwork and professional networks. The informal learning experience with professionals helps students relate their classroom learning to real experience, which is critical for their sense-making, hence they are more likely to engage in the classroom.

Secondly, dealing with sceptical views on the effectiveness of a TA approach, we need to disseminate the TA principles and tools to a broader audience and create open channels to receive constructive feedback. I share examples of good practice to change the conservative attitude in the conventional institutions towards the use of TA approach. For example, in the course development stage, I contributed my module design as an example to demonstrate the use of team-orientated experiential learning approaches and reflective assignment strategy (as some of the principles and methodology of TA) to increase the classroom interaction and enhance student skills. In addition, I took the opportunity of student events, management observation, and staff teaching conferences to organize workshops in collaboration with institutions adopting full TA approaches to stimulate interests, discuss support and receive feedback. For instance, in those workshops, I invited students from some TA programmes to organize online coaching sessions with my students so as to improve their team performance. In our entrepreneurship week, TA students were invited to campus to collaborate with our students for business challenges. These small attempts at gradually introducing TA become a vehicle to devise transitional culture within an entrepreneurship programme to prepare the conventional audiences for more radical TA approaches such as dialectical strategy. This is more probable to be accepted and get supported in the long-term operation.

Dialectical resolution strategy

In contrast to transitional resolution strategy, dialectical resolution strategy shall be adopted *"when resolution occurs not through change-over but by balancing two competing interests...The conflict was not resolved by changing from one logic to another, but rather by synthesizing both sides and finding a combinational balance. Thus, dialectical resolution involves mindfully balancing between competing logics rather than taking them as if in a black-white dichotomy"* (Asangansi, 2012, p. 18). Adopting TA approach at a module level would encounter the great challenge of students being recruited for a conventional programme in terms of the expected learning behaviours. A common problem is that we do not often have much of liberty to recruit independent learners that are likely to fit in the full TA programmes. My resolution to this is to alleviate this tension by creatively combining resources from both communities and balancing the level of intervention in the teaching and the expected self-management in the student learning.

First, the experiential learning principle of TA has the advantage to enrich student experience of entrepreneurial practice in the post-graduate level entrepreneurship programme. It is important to follow the principle of TA in the experiential design, such as learn by doing in the student-led team projects. However, we shall be more sensible to introduce less conventional TA teaching and learning methods to students who are often not the independent learners we purposively recruit into TA programmes. It is therefore sensible not to directly assess their learning outcomes against their performance applying TA principles or tools. I, therefore, adopted lightweight teams approach that *"are class teams in which the team members have little or no direct impact on each other's final grades, yet where there is a significant component of peer teaching, peer learning, and long term socialisation built into the curriculum"* (Latulipe et al., 2015, p. 392). For example, I created team-based business challenges for my students to be coached by students from TA institutions.

According to my experience, this hybrid approach has caused less tension and confusion among students and other colleagues who are used to conventional teaching approaches. Remaining in the neutral position is helpful for a TA educator to build trust from sceptical audiences who are unfamiliar with the purpose of TA approaches, which eventually benefit them when gaining new distinctive entrepreneurial learning experience. This learning opportunity severs to challenge students on their assumption of entrepreneurship and their learning style. This often leads to enhance student ability to have critical thinking and reflection skills, which is more in line with the postgraduate level of learning outcomes in comparison to undergraduate. For these types of hybrid approaches, I do not recommend measuring individual students' performance from team projects, as it is critical to stress reflective learning in the assessment strategy to guide students on embodying the learning in the construction of entrepreneurial identities. To encourage certain level of self-learning and self-management in the hybrid design it is important to supplement the conventional programmes to achieve higher level of entrepreneurial learning by emphasizing the mindset and skills defined by the Quality Assurance Agency (QAA) for Higher Education in the UK (QAA, 2018). In the students' reflection on their team performance to pitch social venture ideas to an accelerator programme, they have seen *the strength of team* and learned *collaborative leadership,* for which they come to realize that t*he importance of process to build a strong team.* Evidently, the hybrid approach does not undermine the success of TA to enhance students' understanding of entrepreneurship by actions and team leadership.

Secondly, the successful implementation of TA requires us to think creatively in mobilizing resources from both TA community and the conventional institution to create collaboration opportunities. The recent rapid development of simulation tools and remote working platforms provide resolutions for educators to overcome the constraints of conventional institutional structure to introduce experiential design for entrepreneurial learning, such as timetabling, distance, and resources. My experience is to have the experiential project operated on the one-term basis and online. For example, I have created an online international learning project for students to practice entrepreneurship with TA students. Because the full TA model has the strength of being flexible to accommodate other conventional programmes, the collaboration approach is a good cost-effective way to achieve impact. In addition, some online platforms, such as *Crowdfunder*, are a less resource-demanding simulation tool to be used for experiential learning that could have the same impact. The hybrid approach of combing TA with conventional pedagogy is not only allowing TA to co-exist with other conventional modules but also to create opportunities to share TA networking resources with other conventional modules.

Conclusion and discussion

The discourse in the open definition of entrepreneurship education has left room for scholarly discussion to review the scope of teaching and learning practice. This has motivated some entrepreneurship educators to move from conventional content teaching, and devote to teaching approaches that enable mindset changes, skills learning, and competence enhancement. There is a calling in literature and in practice to examine how individual learners actually learn with experiential learning programme designs, such as TA. This could lead entrepreneurship educators and instructors to better explain their philosophical posture and roles in EE. However, meeting such aspiration for entrepreneurship education presents challenges to a strong continuum of established institutions that practice EE in the conventional fashion. This is not to mention the challenges of implementation if there is a radically innovative programme in the spectrum of experiential learning, such as the TA model.

We shall not be constrained by sceptical views and temporal obstacles to show the value of TA as alternative approach to conventional pedagogy. Even though within the TA community many of us believe that its teaching and learning models work integrally as a coherent whole, we shall question the feasibility of the TA for a high-education context outside its originality (Tosey et al., 2015). Hence, we shall enquire on the practicality of modifying or transforming TA to be more adaptive to other High Education contexts, such as the UK High Education sector, that, with its conventional approach has historical success and renowned reputation of quality assurance. A hostile or turbulent environment or inhibiting processes could either suppress learning or spur it if the content is strong and students have the right instructors (Krueger, 2015).

On the other hand, we need to be mindful in negotiating the role that TA plays in conventional institutional environments while not undermining the value of the TA model as alternative and innovative approach to supplement the conventional pedagogy. The necessity of TA model seeking an experiential approach to learning and coaching student-led team projects shall not be eliminated. An example of this is the likelihood for students to own businesses, which would be discarded in other contexts due to the institution's insurance and risk management requirements. This would remove a dynamic that lies at the heart of the Team Academy. We shall not give up on encouraging students who have some, albeit limited, experience of entrepreneurship to recognize a need of developing competence and learn in different educational approaches. The most essential role of the team is to provide students opportunities to learn by doing and enhance their skills, such as creativity, innovation, leadership, communication, team working, planning, and decision-making.

According to Neck and Corbett (2018), EE programme from old-school pedagogical approaches to the ideal heutagogy approach varies on desired educational outcomes, centre of learning, instructor role, and student role. For a community of practice, we do not pursue *"one best way in EE, nor should there be"* (Neck and Corbett, 2018, p. 31), but encourage entrepreneurship educators to embrace on a continuum depending on programming goals, student populations, and university resources. Neck and Corbett, (2018) suggest alignment between heutagogy in the most dedicated and mature adult learning, which provides the philosophical stance to promote the TA model in the conventional pedagogy, whereas andragogy is adult learning but with more guidance. It is empirically evident that EE today aligns mostly with andragogy and, in some cases, heutagogy. The idea of pedagogy, however, represents EE of the past. This is also inference from my reflection on the experience of implementing the TA model in a UK conventional university postgraduate course.

Accordingly, this chapter proposes a strategy of resolving institutional conflicts between the TA heutagogical approaches and the conventional pedagogical approaches as consisting of three possible strategies - deinstitutionalization, transitional and dialectical resolutions (in Table 6.1). Largely, we have seen deinstitutionalization as the common resolution strategy to implement TA, which inevitably creates tension and confusion as replacement to erode the conventional institutional structure and culture. However, my experience suggests that there are alternative strategies. Particularly, by reflecting on my own experience, I propose the need to pay attention to institutional conflicts in EE and incrementally build up strategies to introduce TA to the conventional institutional environment. I have highlighted how the changes taking place as the implementing process is fuelled by institutional conflicts and the drive to resolve them.

It is critical that we reckon, fundamentally, the principles of TA model and the conventional pedagogy sometimes conflict, which inevitably increases the risk of implementation failure. On the other hand, constraints in the conventional pedagogy structure and culture can be perceived as a major enabler and driver for improving the flexibility of TA model and resolving the issue of lacking legitimacy and critical stance. The case in this chapter confirms what is suggested in the literature of conflict resolution strategy that resolution as the reaction to challenges is emerging in the process of learning by the need to resolve conflicts (Asangansi, 2012). For example, the transitional resolution applied in the initial stage of TA implementation creates receptible attitude towards the possibility of TA approached to be fully implemented. To perceive conventional institutional constraints as the need for change motivates us to be innovative and solve problems. Hence, to be critical with our approaches and challenging assumptions (regardless of whether it is TA or conventional pedagogy) is a necessary change management phase we shall go through for promoting the TA brand.

I suggest the key to successful TA implementation is to be reflective and flexible towards our practice, which is a major step to deal with the issues of lacking legitimacy and critical stance. In this chapter, I provided common views of challenges that educator encounters in the TA practice and my limited experience of finding effective resolutions in the specific context. The use of a single case has limitations to generalize the conclusion, but my inference is based on relevant review of literature. This case study has revealed a few common issues others might have when adopting some of key TA principles, such as learn by doing and coaching student-led team projects. My findings and reflection from this case about the hybrid design (Table 6.1) have the underpinning of EE literature and the framework of conflicting institutional resolution strategy. Hence, the suggestions of hybrid design can be taken broadly to assist the application of TA in similar EE programmes where the institutional conflicts play a role.

References

Asangansi, I. (2012). Understanding HMIS implementation in a developing country ministry of health context-an institutional logics perspective. *Online Journal of Public Health Informatics, 4*(3). DOI: 10.5210/ojphi.v4i3.4302.

Blackwood, T., Round, A., Pugalis, L., & Hatt, L. (2015). Making sense of learning: Insights from an experientially-based undergraduate entrepreneurship programme. *Industry and Higher Education, 29*(6), pp. 445–457. DOI:10.5367/ihe.2015.0278.

Donnellon, A., Ollila, S., & Middleton, K. W. (2014). Constructing entrepreneurial identity in entrepreneurship education. *The International Journal of Management Education, 12*(3), pp. 490–499. DOI: 10.1016/j.ijme.2014.05.004.

Halttunen, J. (2006). Team Academy–Award winning entrepreneurship education from Jyvaskyla, Finland. *In Presentation given at OECD/IMHE Conference, Copenhagen, Denmark*. DOI: http://www.oecd.org/education/imhe/37544053.pdf.

Fayolle, A. (2018). Personal views on the future of entrepreneurship education. In *A research agenda for entrepreneurship education*. Edward Elgar Publishing. DOI: 10.4337/9781786432919.00013.

Latulipe, C., Long, N. B., & Seminario, C. E. (2015, February). Structuring flipped classes with lightweight teams and gamification. In *Proceedings of the 46th ACM Technical Symposium on Computer Science Education* (pp. 392–397). DOI: 10.1145/2676723.2677240.

Krueger, N., & Welpe, I. (2014). Neuroentrepreneurship: what can entrepreneurship learn from neuroscience? In *Annals of Entrepreneurship Education and Pedagogy*, 2014. Edward Elgar Publishing.

Leinonen, N., Partanen, J., Palviainen, P., & Gates, M. (2004). *Team Academy: A true story of a community that learns by doing*. PS-kustannus. DOI: http://661112983.guireadjimu.xyz/.

Krueger, N. F. (2009). The microfoundations of entrepreneurial learning and... education: The experiential essence of entrepreneurial cognition. *Handbook of university-wide entrepreneurship education*, pp. 35–59.

Krueger, N. F. (2015). Part 1- The entrepreneurial mindset, entrepreneurial education in practice. *Entrepreneurship360 Thematic Paper is the Part of ODCD LEED's Work Programme on Skills for Entrepreneurship*. DOI: http://www.oecd.org/cfe/leed/skills-for-entrepreneurship.htm.

Neck, H. M., & Corbett, A. C. (2018). The scholarship of teaching and learning entrepreneurship. *Entrepreneurship Education and Pedagogy*, *1*(1), pp. 8–41. DOI: 10.1177/2515127417737286.

Tosey, P., Dhaliwal, S., & Hassinen, J. (2015). The Finnish Team Academy model: Implications for management education. *Management Learning*, *46*(2), pp. 175–194. DOI: 10.1177/1350507613498334.

QAA (2018). *Enterprise and Entrepreneurship Education: Guidance for UK higher education providers*. Higher Education.

7 How to Develop Team Coaches at Team Academy

Different Contexts, Multiple Paths

Gabriel Faerstein

Introduction

Since their inception in 1993, Team Academy's educational model, methods, and philosophy have inspired and contributed to the development of dozens of different programmes across the globe. As explored throughout this series of books, Team Academy (TA) programmes exist in different shapes, sizes, and contexts. They are found within traditional universities, as independent programmes, accredited bachelor's, master's, and more. This diversity brings different methods, learning points and approaches to developing both team-entrepreneurs (team learners in TA programmes) and Team Coaches.

Throughout its multiple applications, the Team Coach is one of the most important roles within the TA educational model. Team Coaches are responsible for supporting and guiding the team and individual members by facilitating learning, reflection, and entrepreneurial development. Although team coaching is a cornerstone of the TA methods, little research on the activity is available.

As a Team Coach at TA Amsterdam, I've both faced the steep learning curve and observed from my fellow team coaches the challenge to adapt to the TA system, even for experienced professionals. Although Team Coach training & development programmes are provided within the TA international network, they are not always accessible or adapt their methodology to other contexts. My motivation to develop this research comes from my own need to better understand the theoretical foundation behind my practice and to further develop into a successful Team Coach. Questions that will be explored are: What are the competencies of a successful Team Coach? What skills, knowledge, and tools are required to better support team entrepreneurs? And, finally, what is the best way to learn and develop as

DOI: 10.4324/9781003163114-8

a Team Coach? An integrative framework that answers these questions is needed, to support myself and others in their learning journey towards successful team coaching at TA.

A mixed-methods study was undertaken to investigate TA programmes in different contexts: Tiimiakatemia Global; Tiimiakatemia Jyväskylä (Finland), Proakatemia Tampere (Finland), Akatemia (UK), and Northumbria University Newcastle (UK). A survey was used in April 2018 to test Schwab's list of Team Coach success factors, with 28 respondents from the international network of TA Team Coaches. Insights were enriched by semi-structured interviews held between April and May 2018 with 11 Team Coaches, and observations during two field visits to Tiimiakatemia and Proakatemia, in Finland. Existing literature was explored leading to the use of James' (2017) and James et al. (2020) framework for Team Coaching for the theoretical understanding of the practice.

Different characteristics for Team Coach Success will be addressed throughout this chapter, as well as insights on the learning process of team coaching. Findings are used to propose an explorative framework for Team Coach development in the TA context, supporting the expansion of the TA educational model (Figure 7.1).

Exploring team coaching: A challenging field of research

Within the TA network, relatively few academic studies have been published to date. Practitioner publications like *The Team Coach's*

Figure 7.1 Team coach success: Different contexts, multiple paths.
Source: Author's own.

Best Tools (Partanen & Myyrä, 2012), and *How to grow into a team-preneur* (Lehtonen, 2013) are the foundation of this school of thought and share the TA methods. The TA method has drawn from multiple disciplines and theories, most of which target organizations, to create its own models. Research developed by Ruuska and Krawczyk (2013) and Tosey et al (2013) further explore TA's pedagogical model and exposes its' roots in learning by doing, radical constructivism, and exploratory learning. Other publications focus on applying the TA model to different contexts and locations (Jussila & Fowle, 2016; Tosey, Dhaliwal, & Hassinen, 2013; Nevalainen & Maijala, 2012). These studies give some insight into the role of the Team Coach within the context but do not focus on deeper academic exploration of the activity itself.

Looking outside of the TA context, Team Coaching as a field of study lacks theoretical rigour. As observed by several researchers, literature around the topic is practitioner-led and lacks empirical studies – creating a competitive field of conflicting and intersecting theories and models, asking for further integration of theory and practice (James, 2017).

Exploring existing definitions for the activity, the work of Joanne James, *Towards a metaphorical framework for Team Coaching: an autoethnography* (2017), and her holistic understanding of what happens during the Team Coaching activity were considered relevant to the TA context:

> *"A collaborative developmental alliance with an organizational team that contributes to the team's performance over time, through effective teamwork behaviours, trusting and respectful relationships and collective capacity for learning, innovation and change"* (James, 2017, p. 233).

James' work is further developed in *A framework of modes of awareness for team coaching practice"* (2020) and integrates multiple streams of theories and practice into one conceptual framework, containing four separate metaphors and modes of awareness for Team Coaching. Her work shines a light on the dangers of defining Team Coaching without taking into consideration the context in which it is applied. Her four metaphors and modes of awareness (Team as Machine, Team as Family, Team as Ecosystem, and Team and Coach in Wonderland) serve as different lenses, each rooted in its own approaches and theoretical perspectives (Table 7.1).

Table 7.1 A framework of modes of awareness for team coaching practice

Mode of awareness	Focus of noticing and sense-making suggested by this mode	Indicative Theoretical perspectives underpinning this mode	Coaching approaches suggested by this mode
Machine	A functional mode of noticing and sense-making	Elements of team effectiveness (Wageman et al., 2005) Process-driven approach (Carr and Peters, 2013)	Use team diagnostics to develop shared team language and develop effective behaviours; Clarify purpose, process and outcomes
Family	A relational mode of noticing and sense-making	Group behaviours (Bion, 1961; Thornton, 2016) Team cohesion (Salas et al., 2015). Psychological safety (Edmondson, 1999) Creating conditions for dialogue (Lowe, 2004)	Noticing patterns of behaviour; Sharing personal narratives; Appreciating individual contribution; Holding a safe space
Ecosystem	A systemic mode of noticing and sense-making	General systems theory (Rousseau, 2015) Complexity theory (Schneider and Somers, 2006) Solution-focused approaches (De Shazer, 1985) Systemic perspectives in TC (Hawkins, 2011; O'Connor and Cavanagh, 2017)	Mapping the territory and stakeholders; Clarify stakeholder expectations; Review purpose and directions
Wonderland	A curious mode of noticing that is open to not making sense	Questioning and coaching as facilitated dialogic reflective learning (Cox, 2013) Social constructionism (Gergen, 2015) Absurdity in organizations (McCabe, 2016)	Dialogue and questions;Modelling openness; Sharing doubt and confusion

Source: James et al. (2020).

These modes of awareness can be used by Team Coaches to better define and navigate their activity, choose their inclination based on their context, and further specialize in it. James' work goes further, proposing techniques, tools and a sample curriculum for Team Coach development focused on each of the metaphors – proving relevant content to the goals of this research.

What matters in team coaching? The most relevant success factors

After defining the activity of Team Coaching, the question arises: When is a Team Coach successful in their practice? Therefore, exploring the most relevant competencies and success factors needed for a Team Coach in the TA context is the second step in this research. Understanding these factors is critical to define goals of a Team Coach development framework and for measuring its success.

According to Tiimiakatemia, the following competencies are essential:

> "Professional Team Coach's Competencies: *Tiimiakatemia® team coach's competency includes such sub-competencies as team and group facilitation, individual learning and performance enhancement, educational design, teamwork and community building. In addition to team coaching competency, each team coach has his own special area of expertise (marketing, sales, engineering, health care, design thinking, social work, etc.) that he uses in conjunction with his team coaching competency*" (Tiimiakatemia, n.d., p. 3).

Tiimiakatemia introduces a variety of expected fields of competence for team coaching and also mentions competencies related to education and learning – an important aspect of the TA context. These competencies are a starting point and introduce the concept of *each coach as a specialist in their own field.*

In search of a more comprehensive list of competencies used to evaluate Team Coaches, one comes across different models (Pliopas, et al. 2014; Clutterbuck 2013; McLean 2012), either focusing on individual coaching characteristics or on a specific line of team coaching.

Franz Schwab, Team Coach at TA Amsterdam and Coach Trainer, developed a list of coach competencies, used as an assessment tool during his coach training programmes. This list was built based on measures of success and capability used by two of the most recognized Dutch coach certifying organizations (*Nobco & StiR*), combined with research by Miles (1959) – team development researcher and group facilitator – and Rob Gras (1980). The list of 40 factors combines both team and individual coaching competencies. These are divided into the different layers of focus they address during the coach-coachee relation. The layers are:

Content: The content is the topic of conversation or the substantive task that the group stands for (Table 7.2). The content is known, it lays on the metaphorical table.

Procedure: The procedure is the way, agreed on or not, in which the discussion topic or the tasks of the group are dealt with (Table 7.3).

Table 7.2 Functions of the coach concerning the content

Success factor

The coach feels confident on a content level.
The coach provides a clear framework for the process.
The coach gives clear explanations of what happens between people when they interact.
The coach is personally present, responding authentically to what is happening at the moment.
People feel comfortable experimenting with their behaviour around this coach.
The coach enables participants to learn from their actions, and learn from analyzing their actions.
The coach regularly gives cognitive clarification about what is happening.
The coach has technical knowledge and knowledge of methodologies.
The coach is open and direct towards others when the situation calls for it.
The coach masters the relevant knowledge about people and interactions.

Source: Schwab (2018).

Table 7.3 Functions of the coach concerning the procedure

Success factor

The coach offers a clear structure for the session.
The coach draws up plans together with the participants.
The coach masters the necessary procedures such as introduction, evaluation, etc.
The coach uses relevant hardware & software to support the learning process.
The coach possesses the skills to facilitate team building, leadership games, etc.
The coach provides methodical help and leads the process of analysis.
The coach masters the skills of observing and giving feedback.
The coach encourages the development of individuals as well as the team and helps to steer in the direction of where the development should go.
The coach confronts and stimulates where necessary.
The coach can organize complex learning experiences.

Source: Schwab (2018).

Interaction: Interaction is the way people interact (Table 7.4). Do people interact and how? Do some people ignore each other? Do proposals of certain people disappear under the table? Is there respect for each other? Is there powerplay? The interaction is usually not addressed.

Feeling - Feelings have a major influence on how people function in a group (Table 7.5). But these feelings are often not the topic of conversation. Only when people know and trust each other well, and if a culture that allows it exists, there will be talk on an emotional level.

The list has been validated as a valuable assessment tool for coaches and Team Coaches that have been through Schwab's coach training in

Table 7.4 Functions of the coach concerning the interaction

Success factor

The coach deals well with all sorts of people regardless of level, position, or education.
The coach shows personal interest and reflects on his/her own behaviour & the behaviour of others.
The coach respects behaviours, habits, and views that are different to his/her own.
The coach has a good eye (and ear) for group processes.
The coach gives attention and is present in a caring manner.
The coach has a strong ability to sense, feel, and perceive.
The coach is seen as someone who can provide help and support.
The coach addresses participants directly.
The coach ensures that as facilitator, he/she still remains a part of the group.
The coach shows non-defensiveness in case of criticism or discomfort.

Source: Schwab (2018).

Table 7.5 Effective coaching on an emotional level

Success factor

The coach feels comfortable in front of groups
The coach considers people to be important
The coach takes emotions seriously
The coach is able to motivate and stimulate change in participants
The coach provides support when necessary.
The coach shows flexibility in his role and is open to the needs of the group & the individual.
Participants feel supported by the coach (valued, understood).
The coach shows sensitivity towards people, behaviour, and resistance.
The coach doesn't take resistance personally.
The coach regularly performs 'here and now' interventions.

Source: Schwab (2018).

the past – but remained untested in the TA context. The introduced concept of layers of focus showed intersections with and potential for future triangulation with James' metaphorical framework for team coaching. Therefore, Schwab's list of Team Coach success factors can be used to define what is relevant when team coaching at TA, but also as an assessment tool by Team Coaches in the future.

Insights: What makes a successful Team Coach?

Team Coach success factors at TA: A relevance analysis

Schwab's list was sent to the international network of Team Coaches to define the most relevant factors for Team Coach success in this context. A ranking and standard deviation analysis based on the 28 answers provided insight towards what the network agrees as the most important factors for Team Coach success at TA.

Twelve success factors were rated by the network as highly relevant to the practice of Team Coaching within TA. These can be used as learning goals for a development programme for Team Coaches, or as an assessment and evaluation tool (Table 7.6.).

Table 7.6 Highly relevant success factors at Team Academy

Success factor	Layer of Focus
The coach respects behaviours, habits, and views that are different from his/her own.	Interaction
The coach considers people to be important.	Feeling
The coach enables participants to learn from their actions and learn from analyzing their actions.	Content
The coach masters the skills of observing and giving feedback.	Procedure
The coach shows personal interest and reflects on his/her own behaviour & the behaviour of others.	Interaction
The coach deals well with all sorts of people regardless of level, position, or education.	Interaction
Participants feel supported by the coach (valued, understood).	Feeling
The coach is personally present, responding authentically to what is happening at the moment.	Content
The coach has a good eye (and ear) for group processes.	Interaction
People feel comfortable experimenting with their behaviour around this coach.	Content
The coach is open and direct towards others when the situation calls for it.	Content
The coach confronts and stimulates where necessary.	Procedure

Source: *Authors' own based on Likert-scale survey results of* Schwab (2018).

What else matters for Team Coach success?

Interviews, observations, and surveys contributed to broaden the understanding of Team Coach success factors at TA. These insights were organized into three clusters: (1) the professional and entrepreneurial background of a successful Team Coach, (2) specific skills and knowledge a good Team Coach must possess to be successful at TA, and (3) the impact of team coaching on team-entrepreneurs and their preferred coaching styles.

1   Professional and Entrepreneurial background

From the 11 interviewed Team Coaches a diversity of experiences and professional backgrounds was observed. Amongst them were designers, human-resources professionals, social sciences researchers, university teachers, project managers in education, ex-military, and more. Most have had a diverse career, with changes in industries and roles.

Specific coaching background and training were common and valued in the UK, where all interviewed Team Coaches had years of experience in the field before joining TA and held accredited certifications. In Finland, previous coaching experience is less common, and most of the interviewed Team Coaches started coaching within the TA context.

Entrepreneurial experience and knowledge are valued throughout the network. All interviewed agreed that a good Team Coach needs to know about business and entrepreneurship. Some state that a Team Coach should run their own business simultaneously with team coaching. It is interesting to point out all interviewed Team Coaches have had entrepreneurial experiences – either before starting coaching at TA or starting businesses whilst team coaching.

The conclusion from all observations and interviews is that a varied professional background amongst the team of Team Coaches is valued above specific expertise, but entrepreneurial experience and knowledge are key. This is an added value towards supporting the team - entrepreneurs, as each Team Coach also serves as an expert in their own field.

2   Skills & knowledge

Different skills and specific required knowledge were observed during this research. Below are the ones that reoccurred the most across interviews.

- *A good Team Coach* understands the team learning process and team dynamics, and their role in supporting it. Essential knowledge: knowledge management cycle and its adaptation to TA (Nonaka et al., 1996; Partanen & Myyrä, 2012), experiential learning (Kolb, 1984), Team Development theories (Tuckman, 1965; Katzenbach & Smith 1993).
- *A good Team Coach* knows how to learn by himself or herself. This is not only about eagerness to learn, but mostly about the capability of the team coach to learn by himself or with the help of those around him.
- *A good Team Coach* knows how to listen, ask questions, and refrain from giving answers.
- *A good Team Coach* understands the system and context he/she is in. This refers to the understanding of the whole system surrounding the team-entrepreneurs: The team, the educational system, the business world, and the different stakeholders.
- *A good Team Coach* fosters psychological safety within the team. The ability of the Team Coach to provide a safe environment, where team entrepreneurs can experiment, make mistakes and learn from them is key to the success of team coaching at TA.

3   Different styles and their impact on team-entrepreneurs

When asked about what makes a good team coach, most team entrepreneurs focused on the type of relationship between the team and their Team Coach. Team entrepreneurs appreciate feeling cared for and being challenged to perform by their coaches, but never to be led. Personal connection and being treated as peers are valued.

The concept of *sitting on your hands*, or letting the teams make their own mistakes and solve their own issues, came up regularly. Even though questioned by some, most team entrepreneurs highlight the value and learning gained when the teams figure things out by themselves.

There were diverging views on how strict the team coaches should be with their teams, how much they intervene or make themselves unnoticed. Observation showed that younger teams ask for more guidance, whereas more experienced teams value their freedom to explore.

When discussing these results with Team Coaches it became clear that this variance in styles is accepted, and even seen as valuable. As stated by the founder of Tiimiakatemia "*A Team Coach's personality becomes their main tool*" (J. Partanen, personal interview, 25 April 2018).

Next, the results from interviews, observations, and the success factors survey results were related to James' framework to define the most applicable Team Coaching metaphors and modes of awareness at TA.

Out of them, *Team as machine* and its performance and outcome-driven goals has been the least observed metaphor. Interestingly, my own experience as Team Coach in Amsterdam shows that goal-focused coaching is a commonly used approach and team performance can be one of the main drivers. The other three metaphorical perspectives were repeatedly observed throughout the network.

Feeling-related success factors are the most agreed upon, followed by interaction-related factors. This shows an inclination from TA Team Coaches to relate to the *Team as Family* and *Team as Ecosystem* metaphors the most. The latter can be seen as the most relevant within TA, touching on the topic of team learning (Senge, 1990) and the systemic view of team coaching (James, 2017), resonating with common practices across the network. Still, based on the diversity observed, all of James' metaphors should be considered as relevant lenses by Team Coaches at TA. This further substantiates James' understanding that all modes of awareness are useful and used by Team Coaches through their practice, based on the demand and context from the teams they coach.

Insights: The learning journey and main barriers for Team Coach success

Exploring the most relevant success factors for team coaching within TA led the research towards existing Team Coach training programmes, self-guided learning experiences, and the biggest challenges Team Coaches face to feel comfortable in their activity. These aspects were researched to provide deeper insight supporting the development of more successful Team Coaches.

How do Team Coaches learn?

When it comes to learning tools and methods used, it is clear that contextual differences play a role. Finnish Team Coaches at the roots of the educational model value and use most of the same learning tools and philosophy as the team-entrepreneurs, and do not put too much weight on accredited courses and certificates besides Team Mastery. In the UK, all interviewed Team Coaches have looked for or been asked to obtain accredited certifications in coaching, valuing traditional forms of coaching education.

When it comes to the initial learning curve and introduction of new Team Coaches to the TA environment, experiences prove it to be a challenge. Team Mastery Programmes are valued by Team Coaches as an introduction to team learning and the underlying philosophy and tools behind TA, but most coaches feel the need for more concrete examples and coaching tools to help develop their practice and ask for a more traditional form of Team Coaching education on top of the learning by doing approach.

Exploring their continuous development, interviewed Team Coaches mostly value the Team Coaches team as the main forum for their development and use TA tools like the learning contract, training sessions, books, and varied external courses to contribute to learning. A notable article on the topic of coach training, *Coach Education and Continuing Professional Development: Experience and Learning to Coach* (Cushion, Armour, & Jones, 2003), states that observing and listening to more experienced coaches is essential for coach development. *Tandem-coaching* (coaching a team together with a more experienced Team Coach) is proposed as a successful technique for learning and development.

Finally, more than half of the interviewed Team Coaches mentioned visiting other TA programmes as a fruitful approach to learn from their practices.

What are the biggest challenges to Team Coach success?

Various challenges were observed throughout the research, like maintaining the balance between team coaching and academic responsibilities, keeping a healthy distance from team entrepreneurs, and dealing with challenging psychological issues within the team. Amongst all, three challenges emerge as the most mentioned:

- Patience; it is hard for Team Coaches not to intervene, and to wait on the impact of their interventions.
- Confidence in being vulnerable; it is hard for Team Coaches to accept the fact they don't know everything and act within this condition.
- Understanding the boundaries of their role and its success.

Developing successful Team Coaches for TA: An exploratory framework

All findings were organized and combined into a flexible framework that can be applied by organizations and Team Coaches around the world in their journey towards development and success. This framework outlines certain learning and development goals for Team

Coaches, theories and knowledge to be acquired, as well as methods to support their learning journey. James' metaphors for team coaching are used to both guide curriculum development within the framework and to help Team Coaches further develop their own style and philosophy. Schwab's list of success factors for team coaching is proposed as a tool to measure and assess Team Coach success and development.

The framework, visualized in the model below, divides Team Coach development into two phases:

- Initial training: An introduction and training programme for new Team Coaches focusing on clarifying their context, learning required models & theories, and starting to practice their new knowledge and skills in a supportive environment.
- Continuous development: A continuous practice of learning that should be installed within the team of Team Coaches. This cycle should support the development of each Team Coach's individual style and team coaching philosophy, as well as try to solve the biggest challenges they come across during their practice (Figure 7.2).

Initial training

To start with, a Team Coach must understand their context. This touches on their role within the larger educational system of TA, the different stakeholders impacting the team-entrepreneurs, and cultural factors coming into play. Then, basic theory and TA learning models

Figure 7.2 model for the learning journey towards Team Coach success.
Source: Author's own.

should be introduced, with the opportunity to learn and practice the most relevant competencies and skills for the job. Enriching this initial training with field visits to other TA contexts can help Team Coaches understand the nuances of their activities and define their way forward.

In this part of the framework, *the most relevant success factors* derived from Schwab's list come to play, as well as James' four metaphors and sample curriculum. Organizations and Team Coaches should use these tools to further build a curriculum based on their own inclination.

This initial training takes into consideration the most successful learning experiences of Team Coaches, indicating that a combination of learning methods is optimal: theoretical sessions enriched by dialogue, experiential learning in the form of workshops and a mentoring and peer-coaching programme are here advised to jump-start the Team Coaches journey towards success. Before a Team Coach gets their own team, coaching together with a more experienced peer is advised as one of the most impactful learning activities (Table 7.7).

Continuous Development

Team Coaching is a life-long development journey, and this journey should not be a lonely one. Team Coaches learn the most in a team where exchange of experiences, constant reflection, and feedback takes place.

The continuous development cycle should happen within the Team Coaches team and focus on tackling the biggest challenges faced by Team Coaches and in facilitating the development of each Team Coach's own style and personality further. This is where the TA learning by doing and team learning models come into play. To develop, Team Coaches must practice what they preach. Tools like the learning contract (Partanen & Myyrä, 2012) and a self-development plan can help Team Coaches tap into self-organized learning, start specializing, and further building their practice.

In this phase, James' framework becomes a tool for Team Coaches to explore their activity in a holistic manner, enriched by both theory and practice.

Measuring success

Measuring Team Coach success was proven a challenge throughout the network during this research. Feedback and reflection sessions are common practice across Team Academies, but there is no common

Table 7.7 Sample initial training curriculum – To be further developed based on context

Development Goals	Methods	Supporting materials and tools
Understanding of local context and system Understanding of role and organizational success factors	Contextual foundation Lectures & Dialogue	Education and Examination Regulation Documents, etc.
Understanding of self-organized learning and team learning processes	Lectures Dialogue Workshops	Team Coach's Best Tools (Partanen & Myyrä, 2012); The fifth discipline (Senge, 1990); Learning contract & development plan
Understanding and practicing the basics of Dialogue	Workshops Learning by doing Tandem-coaching	Dialogue and the art of thinking together (Isaacs, 1999)
Practice of listening skills and asking questions	Peer-coaching Learning by doing	Dialogue and the art of thinking together (Isaacs, 1999)
Theoretical and practical course: Team as Ecosystem	Develop curriculum Self-study Lectures Experiential learning	James' metaphorical framework and sample curriculum (James, 2017) James' mode of awareness for team coaching framework (James et al, 2020)
Defining your own Team Coaching style and philosophy	Self-organized learning Team-learning	Learning contract and development plan (Partanen & Myyrä, 2012);

Source: *Author's own based on results from research combined with the work of* James (2017).

understanding or one tool to track the development and success of Team Coaches.

Team Coach success in the TA context happens on multiple levels and is ultimately defined by the team entrepreneurs' success – being that academic, business-related, personal development, or relationship-driven. To make the framework complete and adaptable to different contexts, the installation of a success measurement and feedback system is advised. This system should take into consideration relevant indicators on the organizational and team levels, leaving the opportunity for organizations to build further. Schwab's success factor list can be further developed and validated, making measuring the success of Team Coaches at TA a tangible practice, enriched by peer and team-entrepreneur assessment.

A path towards Team Coaches' success at TA

At the beginning of this chapter, the need for a framework towards successful team coaching was explored and evidenced. However, building such a framework comes with its challenges. Biggest of all, the diversity of settings and contexts that influence the activity of team coaching in and out of TA. A dynamic framework was needed, providing flexibility and adaptability but also direction to Team Coaches and organizations.

This framework should serve as a flexible guide for organizations interested in preparing and further developing their Team Coaches. The combination of a holistic definition of team coaching, measuring relevant success factors, next to fostering different learning methods are needed to design a successful path for Team Coaches. Simultaneously, this will mean further development of the impact of the TA methodology.

References

Clutterbuck, D. (2013, August 27). *The Competencies of an Effective Team Coach*. Retrieved June 2018, from David Clutterbuck Partnership: http://www.davidclutterbuckpartnership.com/the-competencies-of-an-effective-team-coach/.

Clutterbuck, D. (2013). Time to focus coaching on the team. *Industrial and Commercial Training*, 45(1), pp. 18–22. 10.1108/00197851311296665.

Cushion, C. J., Armour, K. M., & Jones, R. L. (2003). Coach education and continuing professional development: Experience and learning to coach. *Quest*, *55*, pp. 215–230. 10.1080/00336297.2003.10491800.

Gras, R. (1980). *Trainer en therapeut in de groep.* Baexem: Gamma.
James, J. (2017). *Towards a metaphorical framework of team coaching: An autoethnography.* Newcastle: Northumbria University.
James, J., Mavin, S. and Corlett, S. (2020). A framework of modes of awareness for team coaching practice. *International Journal of Evidence-Based Coaching and Mentoring, 18*(2), pp. 4–18. 10.24384/t724-vm40.
Jussila, N., & Fowle, M. (2016). The adoption of a Finnish learning model in the UK. *Proceedings of The 11th European Conference on Innovation and Entrepreneurship* (pp. 194–201). Jyvaskyla: JAMK University of Applied Sciences.
Kolb, D. A. (1984). *Experiential Learning: Experience as the source of learning and development.* Upper Sadle River: Prentice Hall.
Lehtonen, T. (2013). *How to grow into a teampreneur.* Jyvaskyla: JAMK University of Applied Sciences.
McLean, P. (2012). *The completely revised handbook of coaching.* San Francisco: John Willy & Sons.
Miles, M. B. (1959). *Werken met groepen.* Alphen aan den Rijn/Brussels: Publishing House Kluwer Bv.
Nevalainen, T., & Maijala, M. (2012). Creative management in TAMK Proacademy. *Development and Learning in Organizations: An International Journal, 26*(6), pp. 17–19. 10.1108/14777281211272279.
Nonaka, L., Takeuchi, H., & Umemoto, K. (1996). A theory of organizational knowledge creation. International Journal of Technology Management, *11*(7-8), pp. 833–845. 10.1504/IJTM.1996.025472.
Partanen, J., & Myyrä, A. (2012). *The team coachs best tools. Jyväskylä, Finland: Partus.* Jyväskylä, Finland: Partus.
Passmore, Brown, Csigas, & Al. (2017). *The state of play in european coaching & mentoring – executive report.* European Coaching and Mentoring Research Consortium. Henley: EMCC and Henley Business School.
Pliopas, A., Kerr, A., & Sosinski, M. (2014). *Team coaching project.* International Coach Federation.
Ruuska, J., & Krawczyk, P. (2013). Team academy as learning living lab. In European Phenomena of Entrepreneurship Education and Development. University Industry Conference, Amsterdam.
Schwab, F. (2018). *Team coach success factors list.* Internal Schwab Training & Development report: unpublished.
Senge, P. (1990). *The fifth discipline, the art and practice of the learning organization.* New York: Double Day. 10.1002/pfi.4170300510.
Thornton, C. (2010). *Group and team coaching.* Hove: Routledge. 10.4324/9780203852385.
Tiimiakatemia Global (Partus Ltd). (2016). *A few great slides on Tiimiakatemia Method - for progressive and change-minded educators and builders of learning organizations.* Jyvaskyla: Tiimiakatemia Global.

Tiimiakatemia. (n.d.). *Team coach's profession.* Retrieved June 2018, from Tiimiakatemia - We Create Team Coaches: https://tiimiakatemia.com/en/tiimiakatemia/team-coachs-profession/.

Tosey, P., Dhaliwal, S., & Hassinen, J. (2013). The Finnish Team Academy model: Implications for management education. *Management Learning,* *46*(2), pp. 175–194. 10.1177/1350507613498334.

Tuckman, B. W. (1965). Developmental sequence in small groups. *Psychological Bulletin, 63*(6), pp. 384–399. 10.1037/h0022100.

Vagias, W. M. (2006). Likert-type scale response anchors. *Clemson International Institute for Tourism & Research Development.* Clemson University, pp. 4–5.

Wasylyshyn, K. M. (2003). Executive coaching: An outcome study. *Consulting Psychology Journal: Practice and Research, 55*(2), pp. 94. 10.1037/1061-4087.55.2.94.

8 Mondragon Team Academy and LEINN Degree

From an Educational Revolution to a Global Social Innovation Inter-cooperation Network

Jose Mari Luzarraga Monasterio,
Markel Gibert, Berta Lazaro,
Aitor Lizartza, and Berrbizne Urzelai

Introduction

This chapter will be analyzing the case of Mondragon Team Academy (MTA) and the Leadership, Entrepreneurship & Innovation European Bachelor Degree (LEINN), a cooperative teampreneurship experiment started back in January–April 2008 when a team of four intrapreneurs within Mondragon University (MU) started in the traditional village of Oñate at the heart of Mondragon Cooperative Valley with a seed that created the first European official bachelor degree underpinned by Team Academy (TA) methodology.

Today, September 2020, the LEINN degree is run in 13 cities in 4 continents where a community of +2500 Teampreneurs run their team companies. MTA world network serves and operates social innovation team labs run by local strategic partners in all these cities and countries presenting a *team learning by creating* alternative while combining the learning essence of TA with the team-cooperative entrepreneurship of MONDRAGON cooperative experience.

The aim of this chapter is to help both novice and experts in the education and social entrepreneurship field to understand the key elements of this particular case.

Ethos, principles, and practices of MTA

While analyzing the case of MTA-LEINN we observe that there are some leading principles that have been present in this social

DOI: 10.4324/9781003163114-9

entrepreneurship experiment, which, have become a key cornerstone for its success during +12 years and will remain present within MTA's future steps.

- *Principle 1: Walk the talk (lead by example) – First teampreneurs everywhere*

The co-founding members had made it clear that the aim was not to maintain the conventional education's *teacher-professor and student* duality but create a community of learners that use and practice the same team learning tools. We can see this principle in the first mission statement of MTA created by the co-founding team back in June 2008: *We are teampreneurs making our dreams become true creating team learning cooperatives* adding a new dimension and complementing the pre-existing Finnish version *we create teampreneurs* rooted in a team coaches' perspective.

As a network of teampreneurs, every team is self-organized and is born to address a dual goal of *learning* and *creating* as a team. This includes teams and local institutions who start a new MTA Lab in new cities around the world. Similarly, to the first intrapreneurs' team within MU, it has to be an autonomous and self-organized team that assumes the team learning tools and principles but operates locally. Every time that this principle has not been assumed, (usually motivated by educational institutions' organizational control or control based on ownership of the local initiative) sooner or later, the initiative has ended up failing.

- *Principle 2: Transforming mainstream education – To become a real alternative within the system*

MTA as a social venture assumes the Mandela's principle *"Education is the most powerful weapon to change the world"* (Ractliffe, 2017, p. 123) and Karnani's *"Creating opportunities of employment at a reasonable salary is the best way to eradicate poverty"* (Karnani, 2006, p. 28).

This is reflected in both Arizmendiarrieta's (leading founder of MONDRAGON) and Partanen's (leading founder of *TiimiAkatemia*) thinking that emphasized how teampreneurs create team learning cooperatives have a role to transform their local communities by creating employment (Luzarraga et al., 2010).

This principle became explicit both in MTA's mission in 2008 as well as in the updated version in 2017 *We are passionate team entrepreneurs blooming ourselves to transform the world glocally.*

The founding members were clear that the strategy was not to create an alternative education model *outside* the system but a disruptive, innovative, and transformational education model implemented *inside* the system. It took 18 months of hard work, paperwork, and prototypes to assure that the first MTA program was approved by the Spanish Ministry of Education. This way the *Bachelor in Leadership, Entrepreneurship, and Innovation (LEINN)* became in July 2009 the first European official bachelor degree in entrepreneurship and the first worldwide to officially incorporate team entrepreneurship and TA methodology.

The purpose was not to be *the only one* but *the first one* and MTA would commit with its future local partners worldwide to introduce this model in as many countries and accreditation systems as possible.

* *Principle 3: Open network: Worldwide team of teams – Serving the world as global citizens playing locally with soul-partners*

MTA-LEINN has always integrated *thinking globally* with *acting locally*. The 4 founding members already combined 3 nationalities and as *global citizens* were clear that this initiative had the potential and aim to transform education globally, but at the same time they assumed a local commitment (later MTA labs).

This mindset was crystallized by incorporating the *learning journeys* as a crucial academic element within the curriculum. In MTA-LEINN every teampreneur travels with his/her team internationally and on a yearly basis to activate their global mindset and eventually become a *global citizen*[1].

This *team of teams* and *multi-location* mindset was integrated since the beginning, as the first MTA Lab was opened in Irun in September 2009 and the second one in Onate-Mondragon in September 2010. But it was not until later, inspired by Antonio Cancelo[2] and the example of MONDRAGON international multi-localization strategy (Irizar 2006 and Luzarraga 2008) when this strategy became explicit and the founding members of MTA explored the possibility to assist their friends in Amsterdam and in Madrid who were aiming to bring the MTA-LEINN model as a disruptive education solution and social venture for their local communities.

Table 8.1 describes the different MTA labs' creation dates as well as the local partners who run each lab and the programs in each one. All of these labs have MU as the *academic partner* who certifies the

Table 8.1 MTA-LEINN Labs worldwide

MTA Lab - city	Local partner	Year creation	Programs
MTA Irun (BID)	Mondragon Unibertsitatea Enpresagintza S.Coop	2008	LEINN, MINN, Change Maker Lab
MTA Onate	Mondragon Unibertsitatea Enpresagintza S.Coop	2010	LEINN, MINN, TEAMINN Mastery, Change Maker Lab
MTA Madrid	Team Labs S.Coop	2012	LEINN, Master Yourself
MTA Amsterdam	Team Academy Netherlands	2012–2016	LEINN
MTA Bilbao	Mondragon Unibertsitatea Enpresagintza S.Coop - Bilbao Berrikuntza Factoria	2013	LEINN, MINN, Change Maker Lab, Finntech, Platform Coops
MTA Barcelona	Team Labs S.L.	2014	LEINN, Master Yourself
MTA Valencia	Florida Universitaria S.Coop	2014	LEINN
MTA Shanghai (China)	Travelling Univ. TZBZ S.Coop - Xingwei College	2014 (LEINN Intern. starts Sep 2016)	LEINN, MINN, TEAMINN Mastery, Change Maker Lab
MTA Queretaro	Mondragon Mexico	2015–2021	LEINN
MTA Korea	HBM S.Coop - Travelling Univ. TZBZ S.coop	2017 (LEINN Seoul starts Sep 2020)	LEINN, MINN, TEAMINN Mastery, Platform Coops
MTA Puebla	Universidad IBERO Puebla	2019	LEINN, Platform Coops
MTA Berlin	Travelling Univ. TZBZ S.coop - LastTour S.L.	2020	LEINN Arts, Platform Coops

Source: Authors' own.

LEINN European official degree or co-certifies it, as it is the case of the MTA labs in Queretaro, Puebla, and Shanghai where local partners have been assisted and later accredited and certified by their local governments (similarly to the case of LEINN in the Netherlands[3]).

This way MTA's social impact on education aims not only to transform the local education accreditation system in the Basque Country (Spain) but in other countries too. This proves that it is possible to hack for good the education system everywhere assuring that a *changemakers education* based on *teampreneurship* and *team learning by creating* is possible everywhere. This principle connects fully with ASHOKA's[4] *Everyone A Change Maker* framework (Wise, 2020).

The model had an openness and even more *open-source* mindset, but the institutional commitment behind every MTA lab initiative became somehow a burden to embrace fully this *public good* dimension of the whole MTA community.

- *Principle 4: A holistic system committed to assure successful learning experiences – Framing MTA-LEINN Core Ingredients*

The aim of MTA is not just to create an innovative education but to commit to assuring *successful learning experiences* accepting mistakes as a needed ingredient to develop disruptive innovations. MTA-LENN holistic learning experienced is based on a system with core ingredients & activities that define and root this educational innovation. The following chart describes these core ingredients framed by *Institution, Key Area, and Contribution* (Figure 8.1).

Team methodology

The MTA-LEINN educational model is based on teampreneurship embracing the heritage from *TiimiAkatemia* and evolving the original Rocket Model to the LEINN Trainera Model developed in 2008 (MTA, 2020) and to MTA Falkon Model (Luzarraga, 2020; OpenLeinn, 2020) as is described later in this article. The core activity within this methodology is teampreneurs' *team learning by creating* and team coaches teams (TCT) team coaching them.

Knowledge-content and certification

The educational innovation of MTA-LEINN combines *experiential team learning* with *equipping technically* the learners. These knowledge sources enable not only a holistic spectrum of the learner skills and competencies but also the possibility of assuring an official certification.

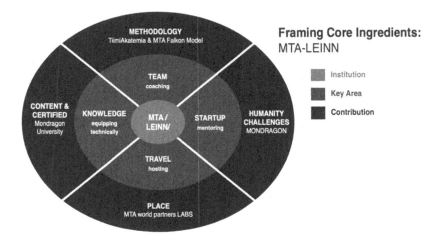

Figure 8.1 Framing MTA-LEINN core ingredients.
Source: Authors' own.

Travel and place

This is a core ingredient that incorporates two learning artefacts happening at MTA ecosystem level:

Learning Journeys, as a crucial element of the whole transformation, process within the LEINN curriculum that enables openness and understanding of different local communities around the world. Within the MTA world, Travelling University (TZBZ S.Coop) is the specialized partner that creates and hosts these learning journeys.

MTA social innovation labs as the physical spaces and environments where transformative learning and creation take place. Within the MTA world there are key referents today such as both the urban labs run in MTA Madrid and Barcelona by the local partner TEAMLABS as well as the *Lasagna Model*[5] in MTA Bilbao BBF (Bilbao Berrikuntza Faktoria) implemented by Mondragon Unibertsitatea and TZBZ in 2014.

Start-up and humanity challenges

MTA-LEINN teampreneurs are devoted to create real companies and cooperatives to transform the world addressing humanity challenges by assuming a *quadruple bottom line* approach, and maximizing their

Social, Economic, Environmental, and Spiritual (or happiness related) impact. They become changemaker teams that create new start-ups as well as transform existing companies as intrapreneurs.

The previous principles and ingredients might help to have an overall understanding of the MTA-LEINN case as an educational social venture. For those willing to have a deeper understanding you may access: MTA Rippling Book Chapter (Schwartz, 2012), Unleashing energy at MTA ecosystem (MTA and Ideas for Change 2019), MTA HundrED award in 2019 (HundrED 2021), or directly accessing to www.OpenLEINN.org/resources.

Historical journey of MTA

The MTA-LEINN experiment, with its 12 years of life, is still a very young phenomenon, said that we are able to identify different phases in this education social venture that may help us to understand the case.

- *Phase 1: Creating MTA-LEINN – Inception and first teams (Jan 2008–Jan 2011)*
  The *need* came from the Business and Management Faculty at MU that wanted a new degree in order to overcome a challenging period by increasing the number of students and embracing a disruptive education innovation. The *will* and motivation came from several sources:
- Aitor Lizartza, Sain Lopez, and Jose Mari Luzarraga, faculty members and researchers at MU and devoted to social entrepreneurship, MONDRAGON cooperative model, and education innovation who were inspired and accepted the challenge to create a new official degree based on *teampreneurship*.
- The Business and Management Faculty Dean Lander Beloki, MU Vice-chancellor Joxe Mari Aizega, and Academic Director Begona Ugarte explored the Finnish Educational Model of *TiimiAkatemia* that was introduced to the Basque Country and MONDRAGON by Peter Senge (MIT professor).
- *Tiimiakatemia* Finland: both Sari Veripää, a teampreneur, and Satu Vainio a team coach at *TiimiAkatemia* Jyvaskyla with the support of Johannes Partnanen and Hanna Walden who were founders of *Tiimiakatemia* and were just starting the first program to train team coaches outside Finland.

In November 2008 Beloki and Ugarte asked Luzarraga to lead the new innovative program. He finally accepted asking for two conditions to be assured: (1) The whole project would be created by a team that would apply and experiment with the same learning tools that would then be implemented in the program, and (2) This team will be self-organized and behave as a social venture within the university (intrapreneurship project), being responsible for achieving their means and resources as well as for making their own decisions. This agreed, the MTA adventure began and the first MTA team was formed to start learning and creating together.

The following 18 months included:

- A trip to Finland where the essence of MTA and LEINN was designed.
- The Regional Government in Gipuzkoa granted 250.000 euros for the project.
- The creation of MTA community first Leading Thoughts by the 4 co-founders.
- The enrolment on Team mastery program to train MTA cofounders and first team coaches.
- The experimentation of several prototypes took place both at Onate and Irun MU campuses where Business Administration conventional students experienced an optional subject called *learning by doing*.
- The creation of LEINN & MTA brand and name.
- A challenging writing process of the first LEINN academic handbook to assure that the degree had a European official certification.
- A Dream storming (Ametsen Ekaitza) youth innovation event to connect with potential candidates, followed by a selection process to identify the first teampreneurs that wanted to be enrolled in the program.

The real action started on the 14th of September 2009 with the very first day of LEINN degree. All the educational programmes and methodology were put into practice and tested by those first 27 teampreneurs that just a few weeks later created the first MTA-LEINN team companies: AKKUA and TAZEBAEZ (later TZBZ. S.Coop).

It is difficult to summarize all the activities and meaningful stories of the first years of the first teams, that very soon would become team companies at MTA Irun (SmartWay and Ego) and at MTA Onate in 2010 (Jumpin and Snatu). In 2010 the MINN Master program

(International Master Program in Intrapreneurship and Open Innovation) was also created.

The best way to explain what these first years meant for these young and corporate teampreneurs, for the cofounders and the MTA team coaches who immediately joined (Larraitz Sein, Bego, and Kaisu), and for the whole MU and Basque education system is to describe how MTA enabled to transform the previous *black and white* educational system to a fresh and *colourful learning experience.* The idea of *"something you are passionate about and good at"* (Robinson, 2009) started to flourish and the transformation began.

• *Phase 2: Opening up – MTA labs model to serve local communities worldwide (Jan 2011–Jan 2018)*

The starting point of the second phase of MTA's history might be September 2011 when MTA was chosen to deliver the opening lecture for the MU Academic year. Instead of a lecture delivered by a professor, MTA played that in a team and 4 *teampreneurs* including the LEINNer M. Gibert, the MINNer A. Garmendia, and the team coaches and cofounders Veripaa and Luzarraga shared the transformation and new beginning that MTA represented. The speech reconnected MTA's present and future with MONDRAGON group's original team cooperatives back in the 1950s.

The recognition and presence of local and regional authorities, as well as potential new partners from outside the Basque Country, became the seed for MTA community to commit to serve local regions (with devoted local teams that shared MTA values and principles) all around the world.

A few months later a team of 4 pioneers (B. Lazaro, F. Lozano, J. Freire, and M. Oliva) and LEINNers (I. Martinez and I. Alkate) started the first initiative of MTA-LEINN in Madrid creating TEAMLABS S.Coop (a cooperative entity later transformed into a Limited Company).

At the same time, a team from MTA agreed to work with the TA in the Netherlands as cofounders and leaders to avoid its closure, implementing LEINN degree in Haarlem-Amsterdam in 2012. This multi-localization strategy faced resistance within the MU Business Faculty board, but MTA cofounders' strategy was finally accepted. As Sain Lopez shared at that time *"after 3 years of MTA success, we are ready to fail with this new risky step, but we cannot accept not to try it first".* In September 2012 the first LEINN teams started both at MTA Madrid lab (Walkinn) and at MTA Amsterdam lab (Fetch).

In 2014, MU Business Faculty organizational structure was modified and MTA was recognized as the formal unit to lead and execute Entrepreneurship programs within Mondragon University. MTA cofounders team unanimously selected Lizartza to be the head of this MU-MTA strategic unit while Luzarraga would lead the international expansion and global support.

Both the academic implementation and the economic feasibility (not enough *teampreneurs* to justify the investments) were challenging. At the same time, the *multi-cultural and multi-located* dimensions increased the complexity of the MTA system. An *MTA world framework* was created in 2015 to define the different agreements (academic, implementation, local lab operations, and MTA world belonging) that needed to take place (OpenLeinn, 2020).

Those MTA labs that shared leading principles have continued to operate and become successful in the long run and new MTA lab initiatives started in cities in Europe (Valencia and Barcelona in 2014) and other countries around the world (China 2015, Mexico 2016, South Korea 2016).

A crucial element in that development has been the TEAMINN Mastery program, created in 2011 together with *Tiimiakatemia* cofounders, a *train of trainers' program* to assure every team coach in MTA goes through a solid on-boarding process including technical and methodological knowledge and an understanding and connection with MTA's leading thoughts. A total of 12 TEAMINN Mastery programs have taken place since then, including 9 in Europe and 3 in Asia with people trained from 12 different nationalities.

Since then and on a yearly basis, the MTA world community Anniversary celebration has taken place where new team coaches from TEAMINN together with the rest of the team coaches and teampreneurs in TA reconnect and rebirth MTA's world-leading thoughts (MTA, 2014, 2017).

• *Phase 3: Consolidation and rebirth – MTA Falkon Era (2018–Today)*

The starting point of this phase was the creation of a working team to develop a new and updated version of the MTA-LEINN educational model, by reviewing the first 10 years of its implementation. There were some crucial elements to address in the new model such as the need to open up the model massively to include new program formats and learners' profiles, the need to fully embrace the learning process, and the use of exponential technologies (AI, blockchain, VR,..), and the need of assuring the wellbeing and personal cultivation of the learners.

This way in June 2019, and after an 11-month process, the new MTA Falkon Model was presented in MTA world 12th anniversary. The new era of 2019–2029 began.

LEINN Degree: From the Rocket model to MTA Falkon era

This section will analyze the LEINN Degree, its academic structure, methodology, and competences, which has been documented to understand the new framework: MTA Falkon Model Presentation (June 2009), MTA Falkon Book (2020), and LEINN Academic Report (July 2020).

The LEINN degree has become the most solid programme that enables to expand TA methods worldwide. It was probably the *boldest* practice assumed by the founding team back in 2008 who wanted to make out of the TA experiment an official degree in Europe. This *creating a product* challenge has enabled the successful implementation of the method within Europe and beyond (Mexico, China, The Netherlands, South Korea,...) over the last 10 years.

• *From the Rocket model to MTA's Falkon era*

The LEINN program was born to respond to the need of promoting innovation, business creation, and the development of entrepreneurial teams in Higher Education. The model is inspired by the Finnish educational model (Partanen, 2012), the educational experience of Mondragon University, and the social and business heritage of Mondragon Cooperative Group. The model was named as *Trainera Model* in relation to the Basque traditional boats.

At the time of celebrating 10 years of LEINN, MTA identified the need and opportunity to carry out a deep assessment of the implementation model of LEINN as a backbone programme for the transformation of young people and catalyst of innovation in diverse socio-cultural contexts.

Previous reflections included the *MTA World Globalizer 2016-17* and *Unleashing MTA-LEINN energy with the team of Ideas for Change (I4C) 2018-2019*. From these, the MTA FALKON Model was created to solve the challenges and weaknesses present in the model, as well as ensure its future.

The analysis identified the following needs, which had to be incorporated into the new model:

1   Integrate the LEINN process into 3 universes or main areas.

- M: Cultivating Changemaker Teams
- T: Impact Start-up development
- A: Technical knowledge and Tools

2   Complement the LEINN model by introducing new learning processes:

- Empathy and diversity
- Personal cultivation and Wellbeing
- Changemaking experiments
- Impact investments with partners and investors
- Emerging Technologies

3   Redefine the team of companions:

- Team Coaches: Companions in the M and in the understanding of the whole learning process
- Business Mentors: Guides in the T
- Legal, financial and technological advice: Companions in the A

In June 2019 this analysis phase finished with the presentation of the new MTA FALKON Model (see Figure 8.2).

MTA worked on the preparation and approval of the new Academic Handbook of the LEINN Degree for UNIBASQ (the Agency for Quality of the Basque Universities System) and the formal implementation of the MTA FALKON Model in LEINN started in the academic year 2020-21. This is the implementation of an educational model that, today, more than ever, is a model that is *Unified and Not Uniform* as it seeks to carry out a *unified* and solid implementation globally but is *not uniform* combining and inviting diversity, creativity, and experimentation by Team Coaches and MTA labs from the whole MTA world community and beyond.

This model represents an open model, not only for the implementation of the LEINN degree but also for the creation of multiple formats and programs that could make the educational model of MTA accessible, always with the focus on empowering, forming, and catalyzing the transformation of young people as agents of change of their local communities globally.

- *MTA universes and modules in the Falkon era*

There are three *universes* in the MTA FALKON Model that correspond to three areas in the process of transformation and training as a team entrepreneur. These are:

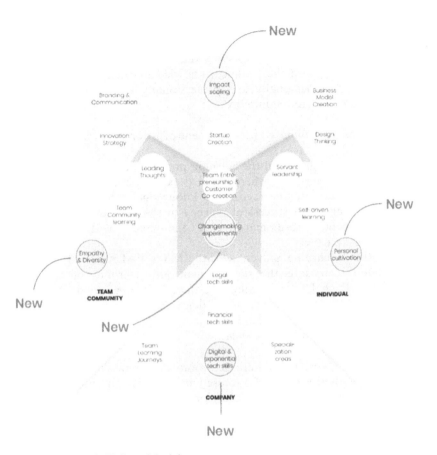

Figure 8.2 MTA Falkon Model.
Source: Luzarraga, 2020.

1   Universe "M": *Cultivating changemaker teams* (Becoming a teampreneur)

In this universe, through the development of various real projects, the identity of the person undertaking the degree evolves to become an *agent of change in a team* (teampreneur). This universe includes two new key learning processes such as *Empathy and Diversity* in the team engine and *Personal Care and Development* in the individual engine.

2   Universe "A": *Technical knowledge and tools* (Equipped with Technical knowledge and tools)

This universe has learning processes that allow the entrepreneur to equip themselves with the technical knowledge and tools that allow them to develop personally and professionally as an entrepreneur, within a team, and in a company.

3   Universe "T": *Impact*   (development of a company with impact)

This universe integrates all the learning processes of creation and development of a company where the real experience *team learning by creating* coexists with the theoretical knowledge and technical tools necessary to ensure a successful journey in the creation of start-ups from its conception to its maturity and the management of investors and strategic partners.

These three learning universes of the MTA FALKON Model are interrelated to ensure the development and learning of the entrepreneur. Each Universe integrates the Modules and subjects that make up the overall structure of the degree.

•   *A model based on competencies*

The new LEINN FALKON era incorporates 21 new skills that, while consistent with the ones in TA used in the previous model, are a milestone since they have been developed specifically for the LEINN Degree.

In Table 8.2 we briefly explain the competency profile of the LEINN Degree:

Competencies are defined as *"the implementation of the set of knowledge, skills, and attitudes of the people who work, to deal with the different tasks related to the profession"* (European Council, E, 2006, p. 13). All of them must respond to the level and quality required in the workplace. These take into account the person, as an individual, and its capabilities to live better, the professional environment, the challenges that they will face, our academic institution, and its heritage and valuable contribution to society.

•   *Commitment to scale team-companies' impact*

The whole system of universes, modules, and competencies establishes the right conditions in order to deepen and re-understand the purpose and

Table 8.2 LEINN competency profile

Leinn general skills	Leinn specific skills	Mondragon University transversal skills
Creative	Global mindset	Cooperative
Open & self-starter	Innovative (& risk mitigators)	Creative & changemaker
Brave & bold	Entrepreneurial leader	Critical thinker & analytical
Aware & future driven	Digital	Life long learner
Team players	Visionary	Global mindset
Honest and transparent	Results & impact-oriented	Resilient
Passion driven	Connected	Aware & socially engaged

Source: Authors' own.

scale of its social-business impact around the globe. Since the launching of the model, more than 1.000 team entrepreneurs have experienced or understood this new model of *learning by creating in teams*.

The pilot and pioneering team to experience this method, *Abora* team, from the first generation of LEINN International, has achieved outstanding results. Registering 3 legal entities in the 4 years of their LEINN International process, they earned 600K euros of investment, as well as developed intrapreneurship projects in organizations such as Ashoka or Fjord in 3 continents.

Embracing the whole new system creates a new reinforcement on the role of the team coach and the team coaches' teams (TCT). The MTA Team Coaching Principles are the main pillars of this key role (see Table 8.3).

Table 8.3 The team coaches way

The team coaches way at MTA
Trust-based accompaniment
Connecting with emotions to foster curiosity
Dialogue, the art of thinking together
The importance of making the right questions
Connect with our passions
The Common in mind
The need for results
The Power of Evaluation and Continuous Feedback
Embracing conflict
Accompany different learning rhythms
Management of uncertainty in entrepreneurship
Your role within the team

Source: Authors' own.

Figure 8.3 MTA World Learning ecosystem.
Source: Author's own.

MTA Today: Results and metrics achieved

MTA is building a network of interdependent MTA labs in 3 continents that share the necessary values and the learning methodology to boost a generation of teampreneurs and glocal changemakers (see Figure 8.3).

Beyond LEINN, here is a brief history about the MTA World Learning ecosystem and programs created:

- *LEINN 2009 - Youngsters 17–25 years old - Until now 2.000 LEINNers*

LEINN bachelor program started in 2009 in Irun with 27 LEINNers reaching 1.000 students in 10 labs in 2021. Around 39% of alumni continue on entrepreneurial activities after two years of graduation, 58% are working on intrapreneurial or innovation-related projects within existing organizations and 97% are employed (youth unemployment rate in 2019 in Spain was around 38%).

- *MINN 2010: Intrapreneurs and executive entrepreneurs 30–50 years old – 300 MINNers*

Beyond creating the *generation of the future*, MTA launched in 2010 MINN (18-month International Master Programme in Intrapreneurship and Open Innovation) aimed at professional leaders, intrapreneurs, business- owners, or start-up entrepreneurs. Many of the MINN alumni have developed new entrepreneurial activity or scaled a current one, while others have led intrapreneurial initiatives (e.g. innovation strategy to open a new production plant, hiring 30 new employees (from 50 to 80), and achieving 80% turnover increase).

- *TEAMINN Mastery 2010: MTA Train of trainers program – 250 team coaches*

In order to prepare Team Coaches to support all MTA different programs, the TEAMINN Mastery, based on the Finnish Team Mastery, a *train the trainers* program has been running in collaboration with *TiimiAkatemia* Finnish partners. During the last 10 years, both MINN and TEAMINN, have been delivered in Europe and Asia, including China, South Korea, and India where more than 400 people have been transformed to become both executive Team Intrapreneurs and MTA Team Coaches.

- *MTA Change Maker Lab 2017: Multi-faculty university students – +300 Youngsters*

In 2017 TZBZ and the network of MTA Korea, launched the first edition of *Change Maker Lab*. The aim is to use MTA's methodology with multidisciplinary university students (from different faculties) in a 5 months program to work together around social entrepreneurship. So far 5 companies have spin-offs of the first pilot this year.

- *MTA Sports 2017: WATS Sports with values – +1000 sports players trained*

In 2017 MTA graduates from LEINN and MINN created WATS with the aim to eradicate violence in football and train sports with values. Until now three programs have been run including a Master program, a trainers' expert course, and a children and families sport values programme reaching +1000 sports players trained.

- *Platform coops now: May 2020 – 850 digital platforms entrepreneurs & 40 international partners*

At a moment where the concentration of big tech companies is skyrocketing, The New School of New York and MTA together with

MONDRAGON group and TZBZ started equipping people to succeed as *cooperative platform* entrepreneurs in a fast-growing gig
economy. This 12-week program, in its 6 months of history has had
over 850 people from more than 50 countries, willing to change the
way entrepreneurship and self-employment are approached.

Other experimental programs such as EKINN GREENpreneurs
2011 – 12-month program for Unemployed professionals – 75
EKINNers, FAMILINN 2016 – Program for families to become
teams – 9 family-teams (29 people) or ABC-Diversity4Equuality 2017
or The FUTURE GAME 2019 (290 people),...

Additionally, +25.000 people have experimented MTA model
during the several projects and workshops conducted by MTA *teampreneurs* during the last 12 years. Nevertheless, the impact goes beyond
figures and percentages: a personal and professional transformation
also occurs. While it is a qualitative measurement, most of the students
who have experienced an MTA program have defined it as a turning
point in their personal and professional lives and actually feel more
equipped to adapt and lead social, economic, and environmental
challenges ahead.

Reflections and concluding remarks

We would like to finish this chapter by sharing 3 main overall learnings
connected with 3 new frontiers that will allow MTA to bloom further
into the future.

1   Open in multiple formats to enable everyone to experience *team
    learning by creating*

LEINN and MTA process has driven transformation within the
people and organizations. It is a life-changing learning process. We
have applied the methodology in more than 20 nationalities (4 continents) and we can assure that it is a model that transforms youth into
not only entrepreneurs or start-up teams that will be economically
successful but also have a positive contribution to humanity with
Economic, Social, Environmental and Happiness (spiritual) impact.

As Peter Senge (TA supporter and MTA China Godfather) shared
with us a few years ago, we need entrepreneurs who do good and do
well (what in Chinese traditional culture call Qi Yejia 企业家), and
what seems to be fascinating is that not only youth from a community
rooted culture as the Basque region or Mondragon valley, but those
from big cities as Madrid or Valencia and even further as Shanghai or

Seoul are also able to be transformed as social entrepreneurs. Senge shared *"the time is over to be Chinese, Americans, Finnish or Basques [...]. We need a new mythos where we as humans operate in a healthy, balanced, and long-term way in the planet as a whole [...]. And vehicles as TA from Jyvaskyla to San Sebastian to Taihu might be a key vehicle to make this new myth a reality"* (Leinn International, 2017).

Still, there are very few youngsters who have the opportunity to experiment with this transformation. Therefore, we must open up and multiply the formats of our programs, the number of universities & education partners, enabling more youngsters to experience it. The change-making skills nurtured with MTA model can be present in any education program worldwide. Prototypes such as the Platform Coops Now program that reach 850 people in 2020 prove that we need to open up the model.

It is our responsibility to open it up and contribute to the *Everyone a Changemaker* framework proposed by Ashoka (Wise, 2020) where everyone has the possibility and right to experience *change-making*. We need to assure that MTA will contribute to nurturing a united vibrant multi-cultural generation on young teampreneurs from all around the world creating solutions for humanity.

2   Accessibility to everyone and specially to the most vulnerable ones

The expansion of the model has mainly been in middle-high economic class regions and locations. The diversity and accessibility on the use of TA methods need to be addressed. In a post COVID19 era where inequality among youth worldwide is growing faster, we need to prioritize and assume the challenge to serve the most vulnerable. There are +500 Million vulnerable youth worldwide including +300 Million NEETs (Neither Education, Employment, or Training) combining both Global South and Marginal North regions.

Few prototypes and projects have been done in the past in MTA such as the prototypes developed by DOT. Scoop in Mauritania training vulnerable youth hand by hand with ILO and in Somalia with UNICEF, the strategic grant system developed by Traveling University & MU in LEINN International to assure accessibility to vulnerable youth from India, Costa Rica, Africa, etc. as well as the SEPUMA project *from trouble makers to changemakers* done with pre-convict bellow 18 years old youngster in South Korea hand by hand with MTA Korea & Ashoka. Or even combining both realities as it is the case of the Africa Basque Challenge developed to connect both South & North in multi-cultural *changemaker* teams.

These projects are not yet mainstream in MTA, and the solidarity with the most vulnerable ones is definitely a *blind spot* that is not addressed strategically in the MTA world. As we traditionally shared recalling Gandhi in our *TiimiAkatemia Global* +25 years of history *"We need to be the change we want to see in the world"* (Leinonen et al., 2004). We need to go a step further and assume Gandhi's *Talisman* (Kumar, 2006) who invite and challenge us to think and serve the most vulnerable.

3   Leading a Human cantered digital transformation, embracing tech for good & wellbeing

Another blind spot in the past has been the *use of digital tools* in the development & implementation of our methodology. We had in the past a clear belief that our learning methods could only be in place in an *artisan offline way*, and although we have been doing several prototypes since 2017, it was with the Covid19 crises that we open up our minds to nurture a blended online-offline learning process that combines a *multi-verse learning process*. We were coaching +1.000 teampreneurs that were not only in 13 MTA labs worldwide but in almost 1000 different places (their homes) with the only possibility of facilitating their learning digitally. We have activated +25 digital prototypes and tools in 10 months and today we are closer to a pure *blended learning* and evolving to create the first *education digital twin* worldwide (see OpenLeinn, 2020).

As Joe Pine shared with us, there are infinite possibilities to nurture learning within multi-verse learning environments (Pine and Korn, 2010). It took us 10 years to acknowledge and understand it.

Within this digital transformation there is the opportunity and need to embrace exponential technologies as well as the *collective augmented intelligence* combining human and machine intelligence (Malone, 2020). Similarly, as we have seen in sports industry, we need to incorporate machine learning and artificial intelligence to combine and complement our understanding and support the development of teampreneurs worldwide.

Within this digital transformation, we will live a re-evolution on the way we have been running MTA programs and there are infinite possibilities ahead to embrace. Strategic steps as the partnership and shared entity by MU, Teamlabs, and Sngular (a +900 tech consultancy firm) or the new Digital LEINN Platform project will enable this transformation.

At the same time, there are limitations and threats associated with the use of these technologies. The use of *tech for good* and the *good use* of technology are crucial. A *personal cultivation and wellbeing* learning process becomes more relevant than ever and we need to prioritize it in this new era.

We will finish with our belief that today more than ever Arizmendiarrieta's message is live: *The world has not been given to us to contemplate but to transform it"* (Arizmendiarreta, 1999, p.31) and what Noam Chomsky said, *"craftsmen can be transformed into artists, people that loved their craft for their own sect and refine it with the self-guided energy and inventiveness, and who in so doing cultivate their own intellectual energies and novel their character and increase their enjoyments, this way humanity will be a novel"* (MTA, 2021).

We believe, as Lazaro usually reminds us, *We have not come this far just to reach this far,* all of this *it is just the beginning* of MTA history and all of us in TA need to open up to serve humanity around the world.

Notes

1 The LEINN program curriculum includes a learning journey in the first year of 5–7 weeks in Europe (Finland, Berlin, or Bristol), second-year 5 weeks in America (San Francisco, Seattle, New York, or Costa Rica), and third-year 12–16 weeks in Asia (China, India, or South Korea).

2 Eroski S. Coop co-founder and MONDRAGON President 2000-2008, who believed that a valid solution for the 2008 social and economic crisis was multiplying MTA labs in every city in Spain and around the world.

3 Back in 2011 the owners and leaders of TA Netherlands asked MTA-MU for support as they had been trying to run a TA program in Haarlem (Amsterdam) for three years without success academically and economically. MTA-MU team agreed to assist them in implementing LEINN there and to support them to get an official Dutch accreditation. After 4 years with 2 generations graduated and an economic and academic solid implementation, and especially motivated by the change in the Dutch company ownership (the new owners did not share MTA's strategic vision), MTA-MU leaders decided to end the partnership.

4 ASHOKA is a pioneering foundation founded in 1981 by Bill Drayton. With +3500 social entrepreneurs: https://www.ashoka.org/en-us/story/new-reality

5 Model that aims to nurture a whole ecosystem of teampreneurship in one single space combining Young teampreneurs (LEINNers), co-workers, early-stage team start-up-teams, disruptive innovation teams within consolidated corporations as well as incubators, acceleration programs, and venture builders.

References

Arizmendiarreta, J.M. (1999) (reprint 1983), *Pensamientos*, Caja Laboral Popular, Mondragon.

European Council, E. (2006). Recommendation of the European Parliament and the Council of 18 December 2006 on key competencies for lifelong learning. *Brussels: Official Journal of the European Union, 30*(12), 2006.

Hundred (2021). *Employability award.* https://hundred.org/en/innovations/mta-world-mondragon-team-academy#f79b9292.

Irizar, I. (2006). *Cooperativas, globalización y deslocalización,* Ed., Arrasate: Mondragon Unibertsitatea.

Karnani A. (2006). *Fortune at the bottom of the pyramid: A mirage.* Ross School of Business, wp 1035, Sep. 2006, University de Michigan.

Kumar, R. (2006). When Gandhi's talisman no longer guides policy considerations: Market, deprivation and education in the age of globalisation. *Social Change, 36*(3), pp. 1–46. 10.1177/004908570603600301.

Leinn International (2017). PETER SENGE | MTA China graduation godfather #MTAworld. *YouTube* [video]. 26 Oct. 2017. https://www.youtube.com/watch?app=desktop&v=jS3ZxperbAs.

Leinonen, N., Partanen, J., Palviainen, P., & Gates, M. (2004). *Team Academy: A true story of a community that learns by doing.* PS-kustannu.

Luzarraga, J. M., Lizartza, A., Piironen, P., Tuominiemi, K., and Kolehmainen, I. (2010). *Emprender socialmente en equipo creando cooperativas. Estudio de dos casos paralelos*: *Partanen-Team Academy y Arizmendiarrieta-MONDRAGON.* GAZE Conference 2010. Donostia.

Luzarraga, J.M. (2008). *Mondragon Multilocalisation strategy: Innovating a human centered globalization,* Arrasate: Mondragon Unibertsitatea.

Luzarraga, J.M. (2020, Apr. 24). MTA FALKON model - LEINN - 2019-29. [Power point slides]. SlideShare. https://www.slideshare.net/jmluzarraga/new-mta-falkon-model-leinn-201929.

Malone, T. W. (2020). How can human-computer "superminds" develop business strategies?. In *The Future of Management in an AI World* (pp. 165–183) Cham: Palgrave Macmillan,.

MTA (2014). *MTA Culturecode: Little things about us.* https://es.slideshare.net/Mondragonteamacademy/litlle-thing-about-mta-january-2014.

MTA (2017). MTA world leading thoughts. https://mtaworld.com/mtaworld/leading-thoughts.

MTA (2020). *Internal meeting notes.* Irun.

MTA (2020). *Teaching guide Degree in Leadership, Entrepreneurship and Innovation 2020-21 (2015 study plan).* https://www.mondragon.edu/documents/20182/84315/LEINN+Guia+Docente+en.pdf/e32f1578-a758-4fe2-a142-cb420f83ab82.

OpenLeinn (2020). *MTA Falkon Book/ MTA world framework/ MTA Team coaching.* http://www.OpenLEINN.org/.

Partanen, J. (2012) *The team coach's best tools.* Jyväskylä, Finland: Partus.

Partanen, T. (2004), *Team Academy the book.* Jyvaskyla.

Pine II, B. J., & Korn, K. C. (2010). *Infinite possibility: Creating customer value on the digital frontier.* Berrett-Koehler Publishers.

Ractliffe, S. (2017). *Oxford essential quotations* (5th Ed.). Oxford University Press. DOI: 10.1093/acref/9780191843730.001.000.

Robinson, K. (2009). *The element: How finding your passion changes everything.* Penguin.

Schwartz, B. (2012). *Rippling: How social entrepreneurs spread innovation throughout the world.* John Wiley & Sons.

Wise (2020). *Everyone a Changemaker Ecosystems: A new framework for the growing up years.* Special Focus: Designing Vibrant and Purposeful Learning Communities. https://www.wise-qatar.org/everyone-a-changemaker-ecosystems-a-new-framework-for-the-growing-up-years/.

Concluding Thoughts: Contributors' Conversation

Berrbizne Urzelai and Elinor Vettraino

Throughout this second book of the *Routledge Focus on Team Academy* series, you will meet a number of researchers, practitioners, and learners all working with the Team Academy model and philosophy of entrepreneurial team learning. What follows is an amalgamation of a number of conversations that have taken place over the development of the *Team Academy in Practice* book, along with responses to some core questions about how TA was spread and implemented around the world. To help focus the thinking about the model, we invited authors to consider responses to questions around the local culture, the institutional barriers, and how the future of TA and its international network might look like in a post COVID19 era. The emerging conversations in this chapter offer some indication of some of the contributors' thoughts about the model and approach.

Berrbizne Urzelai:	I want to start with something that for me was the most important driver to produce this book series, and that has to do with how local culture has shaped and influenced how TA has been established in different forms worldwide. How do you think your local culture has influenced this?
Jose Maria Luzarraga:	the local culture is definitely a crucial element when implementing TA methods, and probably one of the most important elements of TA and teampreneurship success. For me, it is the capacity to adapt locally. I have enjoyed seeing how this phenomenon took place in different cultures. In the Basque Country the deep connection with nature, the women's entrepreneurship power, the deep understanding of community-based enterprises, or the principles within the Basque language, were some of the main local elements. In the case of China, thanks to Master

DOI: 10.4324/9781003163114-10

Nan Huai Chin and Taihu Great Learning centre, the connection with values such as *Qi yejia or community social entrepreneurs*, the importance of personal cultivation, the *losing face* used in learning tools adaptation, or the importance of *perfume education* were some local roots where MTA connected fully while serving young Chinese and creating MTA China.

Berrbizne: So true! And sometimes we do not realize about that until we go abroad, don't we? You touched on a quite relevant point there: Principles, values, and the social entrepreneurship dimension of the programmes. I usually hear this narrative about either you are *business-focused* or *socially focused* and this has always shocked me a bit, maybe because I have been influenced by my education and work experiences in cooperatives that are both economic and socially driven.

Jose Maria: I understand where you are coming from! TA methods are not just an "education methodology or learning tools" but a learning culture with very profound principles and values in place. Values such as *socratic dialogue, democracy, and equal participation,*…In our case in MTA since the very beginning, TA methods merged with the MONDRAGON Cooperative culture, two cultures that share core principles and nurture one another to become stronger.

Elinor Vettraino: Indeed. And this is also reflected in the culture of the institution. I have very different views on this as both universities that I have developed TA programmes in are very different to each other. Bishop Grosseteste University (BGU) is a very small university in a very rural part of the east of England with a reputation locally and regionally as a teacher training institution. As an Anglican university, the ethos and culture are very much about community partnerships, social responsibility, and ethical practice, and the introduction of any form of business programme had been resisted historically because of anxiety around how a course focused on business would map to the values of the institution. The focus for the TA programme had to be very clearly aligned to ethical practice and creating social value as well as financial value. On another hand, the institution I am currently in, Aston University, has a very strong reputation for business activity, not just in the local and regional Birmingham and West Midlands network, but nationally and internationally. Aston also has a very strong incubator system, BSEEN, supported by the Centre for Growth which has a very well-connected network of businesses throughout the region. The local culture for establishing a TA programme has therefore been focused on innovation, developing real-world business practice whilst engaging students in high-quality academic learning. However, because ethical business practice and social responsibility are core to understanding modern business practice, these form very key aspects of the culture created in our TA hub.

Polly Wardle: Actually, for us, this is a key element. Being based at a Charity and in South Bristol, an area of high economic and social deprivation, we find that community and charity are naturally instilled into our TEs. They are based in an environment where the organization is always running projects and educational programmes to inspire and provide opportunity to those who need it. This has shown itself in some of the team companies on the programme, with charity and local community a common theme among their Mission, Vision, Values.

Berrbizne: mmm so this makes me think about something I have been discussing with the team coaches' team in Bristol and that is the dilemma between reflection/process and performance/outcomes. It seems that if you are a social enterprise you do not need to care about performance and finance. And I have the feeling that sometimes we do not push enough on the business performance outcomes. How do you think those institutional cultures reflect in the programme and the way our teampreneurs work?

Lauren Davies: You are right Biz, we need to continue talking about this with the team. I think that there are also differences in legal/structural requirements within both educational systems, e.g. in the UK as students are paying for their education it's not possible to *fire* students from Team Companies and it's more difficult to link assessment to aspects such as financial targets for teams. We have done so in the new programme design to some extent but there is sometimes a challenge around balancing the weighting, in terms of assessment marks, for performance versus reflection on performance (for both team and individual assignments). Both are important aspects but sometimes a stronger leaning towards reflection within assessment criteria means that Team Entrepreneurs may, at the extreme end, develop the belief that it doesn't matter how well they perform, if they meet client's needs etc., as long as they reflect well on their learning.

Berrbizne: Exactly and as a team coach, I often think... When are you going to stop reflecting about what you could have done differently and actually start doing it?

Lauren: I know ... that can be a bit frustrating isn't it? But it's important to get this balance right because reflection on learning (including learning from failure) is a key entrepreneurial skill that we want our TEs to be developing and I feel we wouldn't want to move too far the other way in terms of purely measuring performance and potentially leading to a situation where TEs are afraid to try new things for fear of failure and this being reflected in their marks. However, I believe we need to ensure we are not inadvertently creating a culture where it is acceptable to not follow through on things, not make acceptable levels of progress towards targets, not satisfy the needs of external clients, etc.

Gabriel Faerstein: In the Netherlands, mentionable applications of the practical assessment are the *Money Goal* – Ascending profit goals per year to be acquired by the teams, through entrepreneurial activities – and *Customer Visits* – meetings with potential clients or experts to support the development of projects. These assessments are directly related to ECTS points in our academy.

Lionel Emery: Actually, that is what we should be thinking about: local businesses and entrepreneurs. For us, in Switzerland, the local culture has favoured the emergence of our Team Academy. We have received very positive feedback from many companies that have supported the development of a Team Academy. More and more companies are interested in Team Academy. They collaborate and support our teampreneurs more and more.

Berrbizne: That is great to hear Lionel! Within some institutions, there is this feeling of TA not being *academically rigorous* but at the end of the day we are creating employable and enterprising people, so we should hear what those companies and external organizations say and balance the *theory-practice* pedagogic design accordingly.

Gabriel: Here we have moved from self-organized learning to *guided* self-organized learning. We have made our program into a flexible curriculum with a theoretical program (focused on applying theory into practice) and a practical program made out of entrepreneurial challenges. We have also developed different roles for the program, such as *field experts* and *business coaches*. The first are responsible for providing content and facilitation of workshops in the theoretical program and the latter for providing the teams with in-depth business coaching based on the project needs. Team Academy Amsterdam is an independent institution which means we have not had to adapt to existing universities. Our biggest challenges in establishing our program were related to finding sustainability as a business model and gaining our own accreditation. The biggest challenge for that was achieving the requirements expected from a higher education institution in the Netherlands. This pushed us to create our own format for a bachelor thesis, as well as develop a theoretical curriculum highly focused on practical application.

Lauren: In UWE initially, there were barriers in interpreting the internal quality assurance requirements for programmes, e.g. assessments *under controlled conditions* traditionally meant exams, but this had to be contextualized for TE but now in the revalidation of the new programme we did not face that problem as by this point it is well-established and is often viewed as a flagship programme in UWE.

Berrbizne: That in itself it's a massive step forward. We have raised an important dilemma here people... the point of individual vs. team assignments and projects. We started talking about culture and I think culture has a clear impact on how *individually focused* or *team focused* the programmes are in different parts of the world.

Caroline Merdinger-Rumpler: It does! French culture is one of the most individualistic in Europe. Therefore the foundation of TA teamwork is not based on national cultural values and students have almost no experience of teamwork in their school career prior to coming into our TA in Strasbourg. There is a real challenge to take up: that of acculturation of students to a collective and cooperative work...

Gabriel: We are facing the same challenge, Caroline. I personally believe that Dutch culture is naturally individualistic, so working in teams proves a big challenge. We see many of our team entrepreneurs focusing on building their own individual businesses and trying to use the team as a learning team and breaking this natural tendency is a big focus for Team Coaches.

Lauren: I am afraid you are not alone on that!. The UK education system places more emphasis on the individual so the self-directed learning aspect has been emphasized whereas the team dimension is, I think, the most prominent aspect in other countries (e.g. Finland). I think that Finland as a country has a more collectivist culture than the UK and this has an influence. I think this is seen in, for example, a small number of whole Team Company projects and ventures in TA Bristol compared within Finland where, as I understand, this is an expectation for all Team Entrepreneurs. Also, the weighting of team assignments has historically been low within TA Bristol. This has changed with the new programme design in which the Team Company module has an equal weighting to the three individually-focused modules, and a larger weighting overall than in the previous model. However, this still makes up one-quarter of a Team Entrepreneur's overall grade compared to their individual assignments.

Nan Jiang: hmm..... it is all about getting the balance right, that is true. And talking about balance and challenges, do not forget that there are many hybrid models to TA. Our master's programme is an example of it. My approach resulted from the challenging experience of negotiating and carving the space for the TA approach towards the experiential learning in entrepreneurship education.

Gabriel: Yes, it is challenging. One of the most relevant requests and dialogue with the Dutch accreditation body was about the creation of a structured way to assess student progress and quality whilst completing the program – that should comply with the national requirements and European Credit Transfer and Accumulation System (ECTS) grading.

Nan:	Yes, but constraints in the conventional pedagogical culture can be perceived as a major enabler and driver for improving the adaptability of the TA model.
Berrbizne:	That is an interesting point, Nan, as it is difficult to say... this is TA and this is not. There are so many variations that it is true that it is important to maintain some core elements *loyal* to the model.
Jose Maria:	As MTA is present in +13 cities and countries around the world, so we have lived the need of sharing a "core common" and having a deep connection with *each local culture.* Some cultural values are core & common to be shared globally and some are adapted to the local reality. There have been cases where the local culture adaptation was too much and some core cultural & methodological elements were not in place. (trying to create individual companies in TA Netherlands, maintaining the Teacher and University Staff power in Queretaro, ...).
Berrbizne:	That is definitely a challenge. What other barriers did you face when trying to establish the programme or expand it?
Elinor:	At BGU there were challenges in relation to properly marketing the programme and because of that, it was hard to help the world understand what the B(TE) programme was. Also, Lincolnshire is a very rural part of the East-Midlands of England, and although it does have an entrepreneurial culture which is gaining momentum, it isn't necessarily known for supporting entrepreneurial activities so it required a great deal of work to try and establish the concept of entrepreneurial activity, particularly from a university not known for business activity.
Lauren:	at UWE we ran the master's programme for a period but I believe there were not sufficient numbers to make this viable, so I suppose student recruitment was also a challenge here.
Berrbizne:	Oh yes, getting enough students is always a challenge for such niche programmes.
Elinor:	At Aston University, the scope for entrepreneurial activity is vast and our portfolio is supported as part of a suite of provision known as *non-standard* programmes. However, it is true that there are challenges around

finding a niche space in a much larger institution where there are a large number of very successful and highly subscribed programmes; as our programmes are so new it's very difficult to quickly establish them as high cash earners, and indeed they will never be in a place to compete with the large scale programmes. However, we have already grown considerably having only been in operation for 2 years (for the BSc, one for MSc).

Colin Jones: You are doing it amazingly for only being going for just 2 years Elinor! You know that TA is not here in Australia yet. I previously had a conversation about seeking interest/support at my previous institution but the assumed cost (on a per-student basis) was immediately seen as problematic. So there is a lack of awareness (or interest) in the student learning benefits – with a default to traditional costing models prevailing.

Nan: Awareness is so important. The main barriers I faced were dealing with the skeptical attitude towards the TA approach caused by the institutional conflict between pedagogy and heutagogy in EE. The TA methods are perceived as being too radically innovative because its development lacks theoretical underpinning and methodological rigour. We have not yet developed convincing measures to assess the impact of TA methods on entrepreneurial mindset, behaviour, and skills.

Berrbizne: Yes and TA is so different from traditional programmes that if you do not have university executives and managers on board it is difficult to launch or expand a programme.

Olga Bourachni-kova: Not only that, TA is the opposite of the traditional university culture based on the production of knowledge through research and its transmission to students. Coaching a team of students trying to develop individual and collective skillsets through action is a very different enterprise from traditional teaching. The university system was not designed to support this type of commitment. For instance, the contracts of coaches subject to the university's rules are not suited to the needs of the TA program.

Lionel: We were lucky with that. When we launched our Team Academy, we received support from our school management. There was a little resistance from some colleagues and from the head of the program at other partner schools.

Polly: We do not have that pressure either. Being a partner programme we do not find we are caught up in institutional barriers. We have the support and guidance of our institution but the autonomy to make our own decisions on the programme. We plan to organically grow when the demand is there. Being based off-campus in a different environment, yet having the opportunity to engage with the campus and other programmes as and when we want to, is a really enjoyable situation to be in.

Berrbizne: It's like a marriage right? Like it or not we are married with a broader institution so you have to take someone else into account in whatever you do. As in all marriages, you have to work to make it succeed.

Jose Maria: We have learned a lot while implementing MTA in many different "existing institutions" worldwide, such as Mondragon University in the Basque Country, Xingwei College in China, SSKU in South Korea, Universidad IBERO in Puebla (Mexico), Universidad Florida in Valencia (Spain). All the cases have in common the fact that you need to match the success of TA methods & MTA system implementation with the success of the local institution. Most of them expected: Connecting their institution and branding with education innovation & entrepreneurship, becoming a local leader on intrapreneurship education, increasing the number of students directly joining the MTA program, nurturing and training their professors with innovative education methodology, ... As long as the project will satisfy these needs/incentives/goals for the local institutions the support and success are possible. Talking about the local institutions' limitations to overcome there are a few that are common such as (1) the authority of the teacher/professor (as soon as they see this method challenge their power they feel uncomfortable and they questioned/challenge the process), (2) the status quo in basic institution practices such as: "the look and feel" of the rooms, which type of furniture they have or usually purchase, and how is placed in the rooms (classes), the IT systems used and the type of computers and devices, (3) the use of the institution brand and the co-branding strategy with TiimiAkatemia & MTA: All the institutions are self-referral, although they what the final results as shared before, they do not see usually the value of co-branding, (4) the need for empowering teampreneurs, students in the eyes of the local institution, to create real companies. Most institutions feel very concerned about the "image, brand, or even legal impact" of the projects run by them. There are many others that might happen specifically in each institution but the previous ones are some of the core common ones we have found.

Berrbizne: That is such an interesting summary given you worked in partnership with so many other institutions. So where do you see the future of TA through its international collaboration post COVID19? It has been an interesting year, right?

Elinor: When COVID hit, I was in the second semester of only our first team at Aston University and aware that we would have a cohort of first years and master's level students joining us in September who had never experienced the concept of team learning as it manifests in the model. Along with other institutions we created the Global Business Challenge programme which is an entirely virtual, 8-week long programme that is essentially a large-scale business challenge. The participants fed back that the chance to work collaboratively has added tremendously to their confidence, ability to communicate, and their understanding of different cultures. This great experience is about to enter its third iteration and is now sponsored by Akatemia and involves Germany and The Netherlands as well as USA, Ecuador, UK, and Finland, with more organizations and countries joining as it grows. This programme very clearly shows not just the benefit of TA as a model of learning, but also shows how it is possible to develop quality learning experiences virtually in a post COVID world.

Lauren: I think the pandemic has opened up our mindset as to what can be achieved remotely through technology and this should make international collaborations more accessible in the future. I think projects like the Global Business Challenge will continue to run in a virtual environment, offering rich learning opportunities for TEs. I think that in-person learning journeys will still take place as the TA environment relies very strongly on face-to-face interactions, but I think this will be complemented with virtual international collaborations that can take place more regularly and/ or informally.

Lionel: Hopefully yes. We would hope that more inter national exchanges could be made between teampreneurs (face-to-face or physical). We would see opportunities for collaboration on projects, learning trips, sharing of learning/experience, participation/ observation in coaching sessions of another team company, etc.

Olga: Yes, Lionel, for me the international TA collaboration can be imagined in a 3-step escalating Commitment: (1) Organizing Mixed Training Sessions, (2)Offering a team the possibility to have a long stay in a foreign TA to run businesses, engage in local projects and profit from local coaching, (3) Creating a common curriculum offering a global learning experience through long stays in different TA.

Polly: We see collaboration and internationalization as an integral part of the ethos of TA. Post COVID we will continue with our routine learning journeys and probably take more gratification and learning from them after 12 months of not being able to engage with this, isn't it? It is clear there is opportunity for national and international collaboration using virtual platforms that are now the norm to use daily, whereas before this would have been an unusual activity to develop. I feel COVID has actually opened our eyes to opportunity when working with others remotely.

Gabriel: That is true. With the initial challenges clearer and tackled, we also begin to understand the opportunities working with virtual teams bring to TA. Sharing practices between different TA programs is more important than ever since all teams and Team Coaches currently face similar challenges and have found a multitude of methods and technological solutions. I see the future of TA international collaboration happening first on an institutional level, sharing practices, and research (with projects like this series of books), and co-leading international projects to foster cross-fertilization of learning between team entrepreneurs.

Nan: I like what you are saying about doing it internally first. The recent rapid development of simulation tools and remote working platforms provide resolutions for us to overcome the constraints of conventional institutional structure. Because the full TA model has the strength of being more flexible to accommodate than the conventional program, the collaboration approach is a good cost-effective way to achieve the impact. The hybrid approach of combining TA with conventional pedagogy will create opportunities to share TA networking resources with other conventional programmes.

Jose Maria: There is no doubt one of those opportunities is the evolution from "offline learning practices" to blended offline-online learning tools and the opportunity within digital platforms and tools to strengthen and spread the use of TA methods. In our case, new strategy projects such as www.OpenLEINN.org to unfold the digital potential and open to the world massively and freely is one of the strategic projects. Similarly the evolution of team coaches' training sessions (Socrates global calls and team coaching sessions hosted by Tiimiaatemia & Partus leaders), as well as full version of Team Mastery Train of trainers programs where new team coaches from all around the world can learn and become Team Academy certified team coaches combining an online and/or offline learning programs indistinctly based on their location and specific needs.

Berrbizne: Exactly, I have been talking about that internally with my team too, as we have partners that need new team coaches and there is potential to run *train the trainers* short programmes too to provide some *immediate* support. I love how we are so positive about it and how we are always wearing the learning glasses to make the most of this year's experience with Covid19 to identify opportunities. Let's see where this (r)evolution takes us! We still have a lot to do to spread the word.

*Aitor
Lizartza:*   TA brings Inspiration and real experience to create and develop a professional and vital project. We are having the perspective of a learner everytime! We need to connect the world's teampreneurs to solve global problems.

*Jose
Maria:*   Yes, and we need to open up the model massively after almost 30 years since Johaness Partanen started Tiimiakatemia in Jyvaskyla, 15 since we started MTA world, and 70 since MONDRAGON cooperative experience started in the Basque Country. We need to move from less than 30 education institutions worldwide using to some extent TA methods, to hundreds or thousands of them. In order to do that we need to evolve the current models used to replicate or extend the use of these methods and develop new ones such as societal platforms, digital platform cooperatives, DisCOs, and others inspired in a *teampreneurship revolution, team learning by creating, teams everywhere, coop-entrepreneurship co-everything fair-everything* frame change. All these strategic steps we need to do together supporting each other and connecting all the strengths and lights that every unit using TA methods has worldwide.

Berrbizne: Amen! Let's keep connected and move this forward. It has been an absolute pleasure to have this conversation with you all but let's keep the ball rolling.

As is quite often the case, at the end of our discussions in this book, the second of the series, we were left with more questions to consider about the future of TA and how that takes form internationally and digitally. Rather than being the end of the story, this is very much part of the journey. Book 1: *Team Academy in Entrepreneurship Education* in this series explores the underpinning philosophy of TA, where it began, and how it relates to the broader team coaching and entrepreneurial learning work taking place. In this book 2: *Team Academy in Practice* we have moved into what TA is in practice, exploring research and narratives from those in the field who are working with and developing academic TA-based programmes of study. Book 3: *Team Academy: Leadership and Teams* will consider how leadership and the concept of teams emerge and are defined in the

TA model. And the final book, Book 4: *Team Academy in Diverse Settings*, considers TA as it appears outside of traditional TA-based settings, considering how TA might work in industry, communities of practice, and beyond. There are many more stories to be told, and certainly more research to be done into this emergent model. Join us to further the conversation!

Index

Printed in the United States
by Baker & Taylor Publisher Services